Hjalmar Hjorth Boyesen

Idyls of Norway

Hjalmar Hjorth Boyesen

Idyls of Norway

ISBN/EAN: 9783743337718

Manufactured in Europe, USA, Canada, Australia, Japa

Cover: Foto ©Andreas Hilbeck / pixelio.de

Manufactured and distributed by brebook publishing software (www.brebook.com)

Hjalmar Hjorth Boyesen

Idyls of Norway

CONTENTS.

	PAGE
Dedication, .	iii
The Lost Hellas,	1
Elegy on A. G. L.,	8
Awake, ...	11
The Minstrel at Castle Garden,	14
Elegy on President Garfield, . .	20

IDYLS OF NORWAY.

Brier-Rose, ...	25
Hilda's Little Hood, . .	37
Thoralf and Synnöv, ...	44
Little Sigrid, ...	50
Marit and I, ...	57
Thora, ...	64

EARL SIGURD'S CHRISTMAS EVE, ETC.

	PAGE
EARL SIGURD'S CHRISTMAS EVE,	79
NORWAY,	92
THE NIXY,	95
AN EVERY-DAY TRAGEDY,	99
THE ELF-MAIDENS,	101

NORSE STAVES.

INTRODUCTION	109
STAVE IN "GUNNAR,"	111
COME, FAIREST MAID,	114
TELL ME, ILKA,	116

SONNETS.

JUNO LUDOVISI,	121
EVOLUTION,	124
TO BAYARD TAYLOR—DEDICATION OF A BIOGRAPHY OF GOETHE,	129
THE SEA,	130
THE AIR,	131

CONTENTS.

TO LILLIE.

	PAGE
I Sat and Gazed into the Burning Sky,	135
I saw the Lily Pale and Perfect Grow,	136
Within the Rose I found a Trembling Tear,	137
How can I Lightly Speak thy Wondrous Name,	138
An Anxious Whisper Steals unto my Ear,	139
Thy Gracious Face I Greet with Glad Surprise,	140
Yes, my Old Self is Dead; and it is Well,	141
If I should Lose Thee, Darling, and Behold,	142
I Saw Thee Drifting, Drifting Far Away,	143
I Wonder oft why God, who is so Good,	144

CALPURNIA.

Prelude,	147
In the Palace of the Cæsars,	149
In the Flavian Arena,	160
In the Catacombs of St. Calixtus,	170

THE LOST HELLAS.

O FOR a breath of myrtle and of bay,
And glints of sunny skies through dark leaves flashing,
And dimpling seas beneath a golden day,
Against the strand with soft susurrus plashing!
And fair nude youths, with shouts and laughter dashing
Along the shining beach in martial play!
And rearing 'gainst the sky their snowy portals,
The temples of the glorious Immortals!

Thus oft thou risest, Hellas, from my soul—
A vision of the happy vernal ages,
When men first strove to read life's mystic scroll,
But with the torch of joy lit up its pages;
When with untroubled front the cheerful sages
Serenely wandered toward their shadowy goal,

And praised the gods in dance of stately measure,
And stooped to pluck the harmless bud of pleasure.

Out of the darkness of the primal night,
Like as a dewy Delos from the ocean,
Thy glory rose—a birthplace for the bright
Sun-god of thought. And freedom, high devotion,
And song, sprung from the fount of pure emotion,
Bloomed in the footsteps of the God of light.
And Night shrank back before the joyous pæan,
And flushed with morning rolled the blue Ægean.

Then on Olympus reigned a beauteous throng :
The heavens' wide arch by wrathful Zeus was shaken ;
Fair Phœbus sped his radiant path along,
The darkling earth from happy sleep to waken ;
And wept when by the timorous nymph forsaken,
His passion breathing in complaining song ;
And kindled in the bard the sacred fire,
And lured sweet music from the silent lyre.

Then teemed the earth with creatures glad and fair;
A calm, benignant god dwelt in each river,
And through the rippling stream a naiad's bare
White limbs would upward faintly flash and quiver;
Through prisoning bark the dryad's sigh would shiver,
Expiring softly on the languorous air;
And strange low notes, that scarce the blunt sense seizes,
Were zephyr voices whispering in the breezes.

Chaste Artemis, who guides the lunar car,
The pale nocturnal vigils ever keeping,
Sped through the silent space from star to star;
And, blushing, stooped to kiss Endymion sleeping.
And Psyche, on the lonely mountain weeping,
Was clasped to Eros' heart and wandered far
To brave dread Cerberus and the Stygian water,
With that sweet, dauntless trust her love had taught her.

On Nature's ample, warmly throbbing breast,
Both god and man and beast reposed securely;

And in one large embrace she closely pressed
The sum of being, myriad-shaped but surely
The self-same life ; she saw the soul rise purely
Forever upward in its groping quest
For nobler forms ; and knew in all creation
The same divinely passionate pulsation.

Thus rose the legends fair, which faintly light
The misty centuries with their pallid glimmer,
Of fauns who roam on Mount Cithairon's height,
Where through the leaves their sunburnt faces shimmer ;
And in cool copses, where the day is dimmer,
You hear the trampling of their herded flight ;
And see the tree-tops wave their progress after,
And hear their shouts of wild, immortal laughter.

The vast and foaming life, the fierce desire
Which pulses hotly through the veins of Nature—
Creative rapture and the breath of fire
Which in exalting blight and slay the creature ;
The forces seething 'neath each placid feature
Of Nature's visage which our awe inspire—

All glow and throb with fervid hope and gladness
In Dionysus and his sacred madness.

Each year the lovely god with vine-wreathed brow
In dreamy transport roves the young earth over;
The faun that gayly swings the thyrsus bough,
The nymph chased hotly by her satyr lover,
The roguish Cupids 'mid the flowers that hover—
All join his clamorous train, and upward now
Sweep storms of voices through the heavens sonorous
With gusts of song and dithyrambic chorus.

But where great Nature guards her secret soul,
Where viewless fountains hum in sylvan closes,
There, leaned against a rugged oak-tree's bole,
Amid the rustling sedges, Pan reposes.
And round about the slumberous sunshine dozes,
While from his pastoral pipe rise sounds of dole;
And through the stillness in the forest reigning,
One hears afar the shrill, sad notes complaining.

Thus, in the olden time, while yet the world
A vale of joy was, and a lovely wonder,

Men plucked the bud within its calyx curled,
Revered the still, sweet life that slept there-
    under;
They did not tear the delicate thing asunder
To see its beauty wantonly unfurled,—
They sat at Nature's feet with awed emotion,
Like children listening to the mighty ocean.

And thus they nobly grew to perfect bloom,
With gaze unclouded, in serene endeavor.
No fever-vision from beyond the tomb
Broke o'er their bright and sunlit pathway ever.
For gently as a kiss came Death to sever
From spirit flesh, and to the realm of gloom
The pallid shades with fearless brow descended
To Hades, by the winged god attended.

Why sorrow, then,—with vain petitions seek
The lofty gods in their abodes eternal?
To live is pleasant, and to be a Greek:
To see the earth in garments fresh and vernal;
To watch the fair youths in their sports diurnal,
To feel against your own a maid's warm cheek,

THE LOST HELLAS.

To see from sculptured shrines the smoke ascending,
And with the clouds and ether vaguely blending.

And sweet it is to hear the noble tongue,
Pure Attic Greek with soft precision spoken!
And ah! to hear its liquid music flung,
In rocking chords and melodies unbroken,
From Homer's stormy harp—the deathless token
That Hellas' Titan soul is strong and young—
Young as the spring that's past, whose name assuages
The gloom and sorrow of the sunless ages.

Her fanes are shattered and her bards are dead,
But, like a flame from ruins, leaps her glory
Up from her sacred dust, its rays to shed
On alien skies of art and song and story.
Her spirit, rising from her temples hoary,
Through barren climes dispersed, has northward fled;
As, though the flower be dead, its breath may hover,
A homeless fragrance sweet, the meadows over.

ELEGY ON A. G. L.

(December 15, 1876.)

I.

I stood at morn, amid tempestuous strife
Of wintry winds, and saw or seemed to see,
All like a dim and cruel pageantry,
Thy gentle presence pass from out my life.
And voices wild and strange rose to the skies,—
The sounds of dolorous greetings, tear-choked sighs
Rang like a quivering echo through my soul,
And back into my solitude I stole;
For then the measure of my grief was rife.
They say, sweet friend, that in that realm enchanted
Where thou hast fled,—upon that unknown shore,
Amid unfading day thy life is planted
To bloom in health and joy forevermore.
But ah, the very thought is fraught with dread;
To me, sweet friend, to me thou still art dead!

II.

At thy deserted chamber long I stood,
What time the wintry daylight westward waned.
There desolation chill, relentless reigned,
And thronging memories the pang renewed.
For all bore here the impress of thy thought,—
A subtle fragrance from thy being caught.
For evermore some essence fugitive
Of thy young voice will linger here and live
About this frame,—these sprigs of briar-wood.
Ah, tell me not then, other friends are left!
It gives but keenness to the sting of grief;
For sadder than all else to hearts bereft
Is the cold vision of time's sure relief.
To-day, O friend, I rather would foresee
A life of sorrow consecrate to thee!

III.

Thine was a spirit, tender, rich, and rare,
And purer than the stainless Northland snow;
Still womanly, whose sympathetic glow
Ennobled all that breathed its finer air.

To me—alas! what thou hast been to me
I cannot tell thee now, though mournfully
I ponder on the riddles dark that meet
My gaze where'er I turn. Thy presence sweet
Still through long years of vigil I may share.
For if from that enchanted spirit-land
Thy healthful thought into my soul may shine
(E'en though thy voice be still, and cold thy hand),
To lift my life and make it pure as thine;
Then, though thy place on earth a void must be,
Beloved friend, thou art not dead to me!

AWAKE!

Wake, my beloved, the young day is treading,
   Blushing and fair, over forest and lake,
Flowering life in its footsteps outspreading—
   Wake, my beloved, awake!

Break the dull sleep; while love's spring-time is dawning,
   Let us drink deep of its fleeting delight!
Under our feet at this moment is yawning
   Dark, the compassionless night.

Love, with its turbulent, mighty pulsation,
   Thrills through my veins like a quickening heat;
All my young life with its strong aspiration,
   All have I thrown at thy feet.

If the wild visions of glory should blind me,
   Reach me thy hand, lest I stumble and fall;

Darkness before me, and darkness behind me,
   Thou art my life and my all.

Sweet 'tis to breathe in the balm of thy presence,
   Sweeter to feel the warm gaze of thine eye,
While the fleet moments with bright effervescence
   Whisper their gladness and die.

Then in the depths of my soul as in slumber,
   Hear I great voices of world-shaking deeds,
And the pale day, with its cares without number,
   Far from my vision recedes.

Ere I had seen thee, how tardily flowing
   Stole from my breast the faint notes of my song;
Now, like spring freshets, their gates overthrowing,
   Roll the strong torrents along.

Pale was my life, and the white mists above me
   Dimmed to my sight the soft splendor of May;
Now, but a glimpse of the hope that you love me
   Lights and illumines my way.

Darkling I stood ; and tumultuous fancies
  Surged through my soul like black billows of
    night ;
Now the wide future, in sun-lit expanses,
  Radiant bursts on my sight.

Dost thou not see the dawn's beckoning finger,
  How the young light, like a full-swelling tide,
Breaks through its flood-gates ? Oh, why dost thou
    linger ?
  Wake, my beloved, my bride !

THE MINSTREL AT CASTLE GARDEN.

Hark, whence come those strange vibrations,
  whence that haunting monotone,
Like a mournful voice in darkness, crooning softly
  and alone,
Breathing melancholy whispers that might move a
  heart of stone?

What lone soul, surcharged with sorrow, voices here
  its weird lament,—
Here where Europe's eager exiles, still with hope
  and strength unspent,
Throng beneath the wide-flung portals of this
  mighty continent?

Hark! methinks that in the music of that gently
  murmured strain
I detect a Norseland cadence, trembling through its
  sad refrain,—

Something wild and vague, awaking strange responses in my brain.

Ah, behold, there sits the minstrel high above the surging throng,
On a heap of chests and boxes, playing dreamily along,
Luring back his vanished Norseland by the tone's enchantment strong!

Well I know those guileless features, mirroring the childlike soul,
And those patient eyes and placid, that disguise nor joy nor dole,
And the sturdy, rough-hewn figure, rugged like a fir-tree's bole.

In his violin whose hollow chambers plaintively resound
Is a hushed metallic tremor—shadow voices, felt not found,
By the louder human bustle to the blunter senses drowned.

How they gently stir within me buried chords that
    long were mute ;
And dim memories, awaking, quiver with a life acute,
Of my youth, with its ideals and the long and vain
    pursuit !

God, the judge, the stern and loving, dwelt among
    my childhood's hills,
And his voice was in the thunder and his whisper in
    the rills ;
Visibly his hand extended in my little joys and ills.

And his eye, so large and placid, kept its watch be-
    hind the cloud ;
Saw that all went right in Norway ; cheered the
    humble, awed the proud ;
And amid the forest stillness oft, methought, he
    spoke aloud.

Avalanches, hail, and lightning sped the message of
    his wrath ;
He destroyed and he relented, spreading like a heal-
    ing bath

Sun and rain to raise the harvest in the devastation's
  path.

Rude, perhaps, though not ignoble, was that calm
  and simple life,
Blooming in idyllic quiet and with hope and prom-
  ise rife,
Sheltered safe from vexing problems and from
  thought's harassing strife.

Hush, the minstrel's mood is changing! He has
  bade the old farewell!
From his sight has Norway faded, with the moun-
  tain-guarded dell
And the legend-haunted forests where the elves and
  nixies dwell.

Through a maze of wildering discords—*presto* and
  prestissimo,—
Runs the bow—a wild *legato* rocking madly to and
  fro,
As if wrestled in the music, hope and longing, joy
  and woe.

Joy has triumphed! See how broadens life beyond
    this moment's bar!
How the future brightens, beckons, wide, refulgent,
    star on star;
And the prairies' rolling harvest glimmers faintly
    from afar.

Blindly hast thou come, O minstrel, like a youth of
    old renowned,
Who his father's asses seeking, by good chance a
    kingdom found;
Awed, I ween, and wonder-stricken, standing scep-
    tred, robed, and crowned.

Thus shalt thou, who bread art seeking, conquer
    boons undreamed, unsought;
Thou shalt learn to doubt and suffer; lose thy peace
    so cheaply bought;
Souls grow strong and blossom only on the battle-
    field of thought.

Thine shall be the larger knowledge which the dar-
    ing age has won;

Thou shalt face the truth, unquailing, though thy faith be all undone.
Bats may blink in dusky corners ; eagles gaze upon the sun.

Creeds may vanish, thrones may totter, empires crumble in decay ;
But the ancient God of Battles is the God of strife alway ;
Who shall bless his foe that wrestles bravely until dawn of day.

ELEGY ON PRESIDENT GARFIELD.

Yea, he is dead whom in its heart the nation
Through anxious summer vigils sadly bore,
And powerless are tears and supplication
To bring our chieftain back forevermore.
The darkness swept him to the shadowy shore,
Where echoes not our voice of lamentation;
In vain the tolling bells ring dirges o'er him,
And nations mourn, united, and deplore him.

How nobly met he, and with heart unquailing,
In stalwart manhood's prime, his bitter doom;
And bravely fought, with faith and cheer unfailing,
The weary fight through endless days of gloom.
Nay, e'en within the shadow of the tomb,
While slowly ebbed his strength and life-blood paling,
His smile lit up the night that deepened round him,
And gentle, fearless, calm, Death's angel found him.

And how, with breathless hope and spirit shaken,
The nation watched beside its martyr's bed,
And saw his life's flame flutter and awaken
With fitful flicker, ere it upward sped.
Though absent, we beheld his fallen head,
Yet by its manly beauty unforsaken,
By dolor wasted, and his eye grow dimmer,
Until the gloom engulfed its last faint glimmer.

His was a vigorous soul, of ampler vision
Than those who blindly grope in honor's quest.
Unnurturéd by Europe's worn tradition,
He sprang, puissant, from the virgin West,
And, suckled at a noble mother's breast,
He drank our soil's stern manhood and ambition,
And rose from humble toil to hights of splendor,
His country's pride and hope and her defender.

Alas! the dart of Death, with cruel fleetness,
Found his great heart, for he was foully slain.
Yet his career was grand. Its incompleteness
Gives it a larger mission and domain;

For vainly he lives not, nor dies in vain,
Whose life is full of valor, light, and sweetness,
And at whose bier a sundered people gather,
To weep as for a common friend and father.

IDYLS OF NORWAY.

BRIER-ROSE.

I.

Said Brier-Rose's mother to the naughty Brier-Rose:
"What *will* become of you, my child, the Lord Almighty knows.
You will not scrub the kettles, and you will not touch the broom;
You never sit a minute still at spinning-wheel or loom."

Thus grumbled in the morning, and grumbled late at eve,
The good-wife as she bustled with pot and tray and sieve;
But Brier-Rose, she laughed and she cocked her dainty head:
"Why, I shall marry, Mother dear," full merrily she said.

"*You* marry, saucy Brier-Rose! The man, he is not
 found
To marry such a worthless wench, these seven
 leagues around."
But Brier-Rose, she laughed and she trilled a merry
 lay:
"Perhaps he'll come, my Mother dear, from eight
 leagues away."

The good-wife with a "humph" and a sigh forsook
 the battle,
And flung her pots and pails about with much vin-
 dictive rattle:
"O Lord, what sin did I commit in youthful days,
 and wild,
That thou hast punished me in age with such a
 wayward child?"

Up stole the girl on tiptoe, so that none her step
 could hear,
And laughing pressed an airy kiss behind the good-
 wife's ear.

And she, as e'er relenting, sighed: "Oh, Heaven
    only knows
Whatever will become of you, my naughty Brier-
    Rose!"

The sun was high and summer sounds were teeming
    in the air;
The clank of scythes, the cricket's whir, and swell-
    ing wood-notes rare,
From field and copse and meadow; and through the
    open door
Sweet, fragrant whiffs of new-mown hay the idle
    breezes bore.

Then Brier-Rose grew pensive, like a bird of
    thoughtful mien,
Whose little life has problems among the branches
    green.
She heard the river brawling where the tide was
    swift and strong,
She heard the summer singing its strange, alluring
    song.

And out she skipped the meadows o'er and gazed
    into the sky;
Her heart o'erbrimmed with gladness, she scarce
    herself knew why,
And to a merry tune she hummed, "Oh, Heaven
    only knows
Whatever will become of the naughty Brier-
    Rose!"

Whene'er a thrifty matron this idle maid es-
    pied,
She shook her head in warning, and scarce her wrath
    could hide;
For girls were made for housewives, for spinning-
    wheel and loom,
And not to drink the sunshine and wild-flower's
    sweet perfume.

And oft the maidens cried, when the Brier-Rose
    went by:
"You cannot knit a stocking, and you cannot make
    a pie."

But Brier-Rose, as was her wont, she cocked her
    curly head :
"But I can sing a pretty song," full merrily she
    said.

And oft the young lads shouted, when they saw the
    maid at play :
"Ho, good-for-nothing Brier-Rose, how do you do
    to-day ?"
Then she shook her tiny fist ; to her cheeks the
    color flew :
"However much you coax me, I'll *never* dance with
    you !"

II.

Thus flew the years light-wingéd over Brier-Rose's
    head,
Till she was twenty summers old and yet remained
    unwed.
And all the parish wondered : "The Lord Almighty
    knows
Whatever will become of that naughty Brier-Rose !"

And while they wondered came the Spring a-dan-
    cing o'er the hills ;
Her breath was warmer than of yore, and all the
    mountain rills,
With their tinkling and their rippling and their
    rushing, filled the air,
And the misty sounds of water forth-welling every-
    where.

And in the valley's depth, like a lusty beast of prey,
The river leaped and roared aloud and tossed its
    mane of spray;
Then hushed again its voice to a softly plashing croon,
As dark it rolled beneath the sun and white beneath
    the moon.

It was a merry sight to see the lumber as it whirled
Adown the tawny eddies that hissed and seethed and
    swirled,
Now shooting through the rapids and, with a reeling
    swing,
Into the foam-crests diving like an animated thing.

But in the narrows of the rocks, where o'er a steep incline
The waters plunged, and wreathed in foam the boughs of birch and pine,
The lads kept watch with shout and song, and sent each straggling beam
A-spinning down the rapids, lest it should lock the stream.

III.

AND yet—methinks I hear it now—wild voices in the night,
A rush of feet, a dog's harsh bark, a torch's flaring light,
And wandering gusts of dampness, and 'round us far and nigh,
A throbbing boom of water like a pulse-beat in the sky.

The dawn just pierced the pallid east with spears of gold and red,
As we, with boat-hooks in our hands, toward the narrows sped.

And terror smote us : for we heard the mighty tree-
    tops sway,
And thunder, as of chariots, and hissing showers of
    spray.

"Now, lads," the sheriff shouted, "you are strong,
    like Norway's rock :
A hundred crowns I give to him who breaks the
    lumber-lock !
For if another hour go by, the angry waters'
    spoil
Our homes will be, and fields, and our weary years
    of toil."

We looked each at the other ; each hoped his neigh-
    bor would
Brave death and danger for his home, as valiant
    Norsemen should.
But at our feet the brawling tide expanded like a
    lake,
And whirling beams came shooting on, and made
    the firm rock quake.

"Two hundred crowns!" the sheriff cried, and
    breathless stood the crowd.
"Two hundred crowns, my bonny lads!" in anxious
    tones and loud.
But not a man came forward, and no one spoke or
    stirred,
And nothing save the thunder of the cataract was
    heard.

But as with trembling hands and with fainting
    hearts we stood,
We spied a little curly head emerging from the
    wood.
We heard a little snatch of a merry little song,
And saw the dainty Brier-Rose come dancing
    through the throng.

An angry murmur rose from the people 'round
    about.
"Fling her into the river!" we heard the matrons
    shout;

"Chase her away, the silly thing; for God himself scarce knows
Why ever he created that worthless Brier-Rose."

Sweet Brier-Rose, she heard their cries; a little pensive smile
Across her visage flitted that might a stone beguile;
And then she gave her pretty head a roguish little cock:
"Hand me a boat-hook, lads," she said; "I think I'll break the lock."

Derisive shouts of laughter broke from throats of young and old:
"Ho! good-for-nothing Brier-Rose, your tongue was ever bold."
And, mockingly, a boat-hook into her hands was flung,
When, lo! into the river's midst with daring leaps she sprung!

We saw her dimly through a mist of dense and
    blinding spray ;
From beam to beam she skipped, like a water-sprite
    at play.
And now and then faint gleams we caught of color
    through the mist :
A crimson waist, a golden head, a little dainty
    wrist.

In terror pressed the people to the margin of the
    hill,
A hundred breaths were bated, a hundred hearts
    stood still.
For, hark ! from out the rapids came a strange and
    creaking sound,
And then a crash of thunder which shook the very
    ground.

The waters hurled the lumber mass down o'er the
    rocky steep.
We heard a muffled rumbling and a rolling in the
    deep ;

We saw a tiny form which the torrent swiftly bore
And flung into the wild abyss, where it was seen no
    more.

Ah, little naughty Brier-Rose, thou couldst nor
    weave nor spin ;
Yet thou couldst do a nobler deed than all thy
    mocking kin ;
For thou hadst courage e'en to die, and by thy death
    to save
A thousand farms and lives from the fury of the
    wave.

And yet the adage lives, in the valley of thy birth,
When wayward children spend their days in heed-
    less play and mirth,
Their mothers say, half smiling, half sighing, "Heav-
    en knows
Whatever will become of the naughty Brier-Rose!"

HILDA'S LITTLE HOOD.

In sooth I have forgotten, for it is long ago,
And winters twelve have hid it beneath their
    shrouds of snow;
And 'tisn't well, the parson says, o'er bygone things
    to brood,
But, sure, it was the strangest tale, this tale of
    Hilda's hood.

For Hilda was a merry maid, and wild as wild could
    be,
Among the parish maidens was none so fair as
    she;
Her eyes they shone with wilful mirth, and like a
    golden flood
Her sunny hair rolled downward from her little
    scarlet hood.

I once was out a-fishing, and, though sturdy at the
    oar,
My arms were growing weaker, and I was far from
    shore;
And angry squalls swept thickly from out the lurid
    skies,
And every landmark that I knew was hidden from
    mine eyes.

The gull's shrill shriek above me, the sea's strong
    bass beneath,
The numbness grew upon me with its chilling touch
    of death,—
And blackness gathered round me; then through
    the night's dark shroud
A clear young voice came swiftly as an arrow cleaves
    the cloud.

It was a voice so mellow, so bright and warm and
    round,
As if a beam of sunshine had been melted into
    sound;

It fell upon my frozen nerves and thawed the
    springs of life ;
I grasped the oar and strove afresh ; it was a bitter
    strife.

The breakers roared about me, but the song took
    bolder flight,
And rose above the darkness like a beacon in the
    night ;
And swift I steered and safely, struck shore, and by
    God's rood,
Through gloom and spray I caught the gleam of
    Hilda's scarlet hood.

The moon athwart the darkness broke a broad and
    misty way,
The dawn grew red beyond the sea and sent abroad
    the day ;
And loud I prayed to God above to help me, if He
    could,
For deep into my soul had pierced that gleam from
    Hilda's hood.

I sought her in the forest, I sought her on the
    strand,
The pine-trees spread their dusky roof, bleak lay
    the glittering sand,
Until one Sabbath morning at the parish church I
    stood,
And saw, amid a throng of maids, the little scarlet
    hood.

Then straight my heart ran riot, and wild my pulses
    flew ;
I strove in vain my flutter and my blushes to sub-
    due ;
"Why, Eric!" laughed a roguish maid, "your
    cheeks are red as blood;"
"It is the shine," another cried, "from Hilda's
    scarlet hood."

I answered not, for 'tis not safe to banter with a
    girl ;
The trees, the church, the belfry danced about me
    in a whirl ;

I was as dizzy as a moth that flutters round the
    flame ;
I turned about, and twirled my cap, but could not
    speak for shame.

But that same Sabbath ev'ning, as I sauntered o'er
    the beach
And cursed that foolish heart of mine for choking
    up my speech,
I spied, half wrapped in shadow at the margin of
    the wood,
The wavy mass of sunshine that broke from Hilda's
    hood.

With quickened breath on tiptoe across the sand I
    stepped ;
Her face was hidden in her lap, as though she mused
    or slept ;
The hood had glided backward o'er the hair that
    downward rolled,
Like some large petal of a flower upon a stream of
    gold.

"Fair Hilda," so I whispered, as I bended to her
 ear;
She started up and smiled at me without surprise or
 fear.
"I love you, Hilda," said I; then in whispers more
 subdued :
" Love me again, or wear no more that little scarlet
 hood."

"Why, Eric," cried she, laughing, "how can you
 talk so wild?
I was confirmed last Easter, half maid and half a
 child,
But since you are so stubborn—no, no; I never
 could—
Unless you guess what's written in my little scarlet
 hood."

"I cannot, fairest Hilda," quoth I with mournful
 mien,
While with my hand I gently, and by the maid unseen,

Snatched from the clustering wavelets the brightly flaming thing,
And saw naught there but stitches small, crosswise meandering.

"There's nothing in your hood, love," I cried with heedless mirth.
"Well," laughed she, "out of nothing God made both heaven and earth;
But since the earth to you and me as heritage was given,
I'll only try to make for you a little bit of heaven."

THORALF AND SYNNÖV.

O, HAVE you been in Gudbrand's dale, where Laag-
 en's mighty flood
Chants evermore its wild refrain unto the listening
 wood?
And have you seen the evening sun on those bright
 glaciers glow,
When valleyward it shoots and darts like shafts
 from elfin bow?

Have you beheld the maidens when the sæter*
 path they tread
With ribbons in their sunny hair and milk-pails on
 their head?
And have you heard the fiddles when they strike
 the lusty dance?
Then you have heard of Synnöv Houg, and of myself perchance.

---

* The sæter is the region in highlands where the Norwegian peas-
ants spend the greater part of the summer, pasturing their cattle.

For Synnöv Houg is lissome as the limber willow spray,
And when you think you hold her fast, and she is yours for aye,
Then like the airy blowball that dances o'er the lea,
She gently through your fingers slips and lightly floateth free.

Then it was last St. John's Eve,—I remember it so well,—
We lads had lit a bonfire in a grass-grown little dell;
And all the pretty maidens were seated in a ring,
And some were telling stories, while the rest were listening;

Till up sprang little Synnöv, and she sang a stave as clear
As the skylark's earliest greeting in the morning of the year;
And I—I hardly knew myself, but up they saw me dart,
For every note of Synnöv's stave went straight unto my heart.

And like the rushing currents that from the glaciers flow,
And down into the sunny bays their icy waters throw,
So streamed my heavy bass-notes through the forests far and wide,
And Synnöv's treble rocked like a feather on the tide.

"My little Synnöv," sang I, "thou art good and very fair."
"And little Thoralf," sang she, "of what you say, beware!"
"My fairest Synnöv," quoth I, "my heart was ever thine,
My homestead and my goodly farm, my herds of lowing kine."

"O Thoralf, dearest Thoralf, if that your meaning be—
If your big heart can hold such a little thing as me,
Then I shall truly tell you if e'er I want a man,
And—you are free to catch me, handsome Thoralf
—if you can!"

And down the hillside ran she, where the tangled thicket weaves
A closely latticed bower with its intertwining leaves,
And through the copse she bounded, light-footed as a hare,
And with her merry laughter rang the forest far and near.

Whenever I beheld little Synnöv, all that year,
She fled from my sight as from hunter's shaft the deer;
I lay awake full half the nights and knew not what to do,
For I loved the little Synnöv so tenderly and true.

Then 'twas a summer even up in the birchen glen,
I sat listening to the cuckoo and the twitter of the wren,
When suddenly above me rang out a silver voice;
It rose above the twittering birds and o'er the river's noise.

There sat my little maid, where the rocks had made
    a seat ;
And tiny crimson flowers grew all around her feet,
And on her yellow locks clung a tiny roguish hood ;
Its edge was made of swan's-down, but the cloth was
    red as blood.

And noiselessly behind her I had stolen through the
    copse.
I cursed the restless birch-trees for rustling in their
    tops ;
How merrily my heart beat ! And forth I leapt in
    haste,
And flung a slender birch-bough around the maiden's waist.

She blushed and she fluttered,—then turned away
    to run,
But straight into my sturdy arms I caught the little
    one.
I put her gently down on the heather at my side,
Where tiny crimson flowers the rocky ledges
    hide.

And as the prisoned birdling, when he knows his
    cage full well,
Pours forth his notes full blithely, and naught his
    mirth can quell,
To little Synnöv, striving in vain my hold to flee,
Turned quick on me her roguish eyes and laughed
    full heartily.

"My little Synnöv," said I, "if I remember right,
'Twas something that you promised me a year ago
    to-night."
Then straight she stayed her laughter and serious
    she grew,
And whispered: "Dearest Thoralf, you promised
    something too."

LITTLE SIGRID.

Little Sigrid, fresh and rosy, was a bonny maid indeed,
Like a blossom fair and fragile, peeping from the dewy mead.

Little Sigrid, fresh and rosy, stood before her father bold;
Blue her eyes were as the heavens, bright her hair as marigold:

"Father dear, 'tis drear and lonely for a maid as fair as I,
Here, unsought by gallant wooers, as a maid to live and die.

"Saddle then thy fleetest chargers, whether good or ill betide,
For a twelvemonth I must leave thee, and in haste to court will ride."

So they saddled steed and palfrey; glad in heart young Sigrid rode,
By her merry train attended, to the gallant king's abode.

"Little Sigrid," so the king spake, "here by Christ the white I swear,
Never yet mine eyes have rested on a maid so wondrous fair."

Little Sigrid, laughing gaily at the young king as he swore,
Blushed the while a deeper crimson than she e'er had blushed before.

Flushed with joy each day ascended from the sea and westward waned,
And in little Sigrid's bosom happiness and gladness reigned;

For she rode with knights and ladies to the chase at peep of morn,
While the merry woods resounded with the blare of fife and horn.

And the night was bright with splendor, music, dance, and feast and play,
Like a golden trail that follows in the wake of parting day.

Quoth the king to little Sigrid,—hot was he with wine and glee :
"I do love thee, little Sigrid ; thou must e'er abide with me."

And the foolish little Sigrid to the king made answer so :
"I'll abide with thee and love thee, share thy joy and share thy woe."

"And the day," the gay king whispered, "that to thee I break my troth,
May'st thou claim my soul, my life-blood, to appease God's righteous wrath."

And long days, from eastward rising, sank in blood beneath the west,
And the maid, once merry-hearted, bore a secret 'neath her breast.

"Hast not heard the merry tidings—how the king, whom weal betide,
Rode abroad through seven kingdoms, rode abroad to seek a bride?—

"How in baking and in brewing they more malt and meal have spent,
Than from Michaelmas to Christmas well might feed a continent?"

Sigrid heard the merry tidings; with a tearless, dimmed amaze
She beheld the young bride coming, saw the halls with lights ablaze,

And with hurried steps and breathless to the river-bank she sped,
Leaped into the silent billows, closing dumbly o'er her head.

Winter blew his icy breath and silvered all the earth with frost:
Spring arose warm-cheeked and blushing, followed by his flowery host,

And Sir Alfred, Sigrid's brother, straight bestrode
    his charger gray,—
Harp in hand, wild ditties singing, rode he to the
    court away.

Far and wide renowned that harp was for its strength
    and rich design ;
It was wrought with strange devices from the earth
    and air and brine.

But the seventh night the weary charger at the
    river's side
Stumbled, and the harp fell moaning down upon the
    darkling tide.

And the soul of little Sigrid, wandering homeless,
    seeking rest,*
Slipped into its hollow chamber, hiding in its sound-
    ing breast.

---

  * It is a very prevalent superstition in Norway, and in many other countries, that the soul continues to haunt the place where the body rests, unless it is buried in consecrated ground.

But Sir Alfred clasped it fiercely, and its tone rose
  on the breeze
Like the voice of one that vainly would his wakeful
  woe appease.

And the king, with court assembled, heard the weird
  lamenting tone :
" Summon swift that goodly harper to the threshold
  of my throne."

Then they summoned young Sir Alfred ; fair to see
  and tall was he,
As he stood with head uplifted in that gallant com-
  pany.

And he touched the harp with cunning ; gently rose
  its tuneful breath.
But the king sat mute and shivered, and his cheeks
  were pale as death.

Alfred smote the harp with fervor ; wildly rang its
  wail of grief—
On his throne the young king quivered,—quivered
  like an aspen leaf.

As the third time o'er the metal with a wary touch
 he sped
Snapt each string with loud resounding—on his
 throne the king lay dead.

Through the courtiers' ranks a shuddering, terror-
 haunted whisper stole :
"It is little Sigrid coming back to claim his faithless
 soul."

MARIT AND I.

Marit at the brook-side sitting, rosy, dimpled, merry-eyed,
Saw her lovely visage trembling in the mirror of the tide,
While between her pretty teeth a golden coil of hair she held ;
Like a shining snake it quivered in the tide, and shrunk and swelled.

And she dipped her dainty fingers deftly in the chilly brook ;
Scarce she minded how her image with the ripples curved and shook ;
Stooping, with a tiny shudder dashed the water in her face ;
O'er her brow and cheeks the dew-drops glistening rolled and fell apace.

Breathless sat I, safely hidden in the tree-top dense and green;
For a maid is ne'er so sweet as when she thinks herself unseen;
And I saw her with a scarlet ribbon tie her braid of hair,
And I swore a silent oath I ne'er had seen a thing more fair.

Now, if you will never breathe it, I will tell you something queer—
Only step a little nearer; let me whisper in your ear:
If you think it was the first time that in this sequestered dell
I beheld the little Marit—well, 'tis scarcely fair to tell.

There within my leafy bower sat I, happy as a king,
And two anxious wrens were flitting round about me twittering,

While I gazed at Marit's image framed in heaven's
    eternal blue,
While the clouds were drifting past it, and the birds
    across it flew.

But anon the smile that hovered in the water stole
    away,
Though the sunshine through the birch-leaves flung
    of light its shimmering spray,
And a breath came floating upward as if some one
    gently sighed,
And at just the self-same moment sighed the image
    in the tide.

Then I heard a mournful whisper: "O thou poor,
    thou pretty face,
Without gold what will avail thee bloom of beauty,
    youth, and grace?
For a maid who has no dower—" and her curly head
    she shook :
It was little Marit speaking to her image in the
    brook.

More I heard not, for the whisper in a shivering
    sigh expired,
And the image in the water looked so sad and sweet
    and tired.
Full of love and full of pity, down I stooped her
    plaint to hear:
I could almost touch the ringlets curling archly
    round her ear.

Nearer, still a little nearer, forth I crept along the
    bough.
Tremblingly her lips were moving, and a cloud rose
    on her brow.
"Precious darling," thought I, "grieve not that
    thou hast no lover found—"
Crash the branch went, and, bewildered, down I
    tumbled on the ground.

Up then sprang the little Marit with a cry of wild
    alarm,
And she gazed as if she dreaded I had come to do
    her harm.

Swift she darted through the bushes, and with stupid wonder mute
Stood I staring blankly after, ere I started in pursuit.

And a merry chase I gave her through the underbrush and copse;
Over fallen trunks and bowlders, on she fled with skips and hops,
Glancing sharply o'er her shoulder when she heard my footsteps' sound,
Dashing on with reckless terror like a deer before the hound.

Hot with zeal I broke my pathway where the clustered boughs were dense,
For I wanted to assure her I intended no offence;
And at last, exhausted, fell she on the greensward quivering,
Sobbing, panting, pleading, weeping, like a wild unreasoning thing.

"Marit," said I, stooping down, "I hardly see why
 you should cry :
There is scarce in all the parish such a harmless lad
 as I ;
And you know I always liked you"—here my voice
 was soft and low.
"No, indeed," she sobbed, in answer—"no, indeed,
 I do not know."

But methought that in her voice there was a touch
 of petulance ;
Through the glistening tears I caught a little shy
 and furtive glance.
Growing bolder then, I clasped her dainty hand full
 tenderly,
Though it made a mock exertion, struggling faintly
 to be free.

"Little Marit," said I, gently, "tell me what has
 grieved you so,
For I heard you sighing sorely at the brook a while
 ago."

"Oh," she said, her sobs subduing, with an air demure and meek—
"Oh, it was that naughty kitten ; he had scratched me on the cheek."

"Nothing worse?" I answered, gayly, while I strove her glance to catch.
"Let me look ; my kiss is healing. May I cure the kitten's scratch?"
And I kissed the burning blushes on her cheeks in heedless glee,
Though the marks of Pussy's scratches were invisible to me.

"O thou poor, thou pretty darling," cried I, frantic with delight,
While she gazed upon me smiling, yet with eyes that tears made bright,
"Let thy beauty be thy dower, and be mine to have and hold ;
For a face as sweet as thou hast needs, in sooth, no frame of gold."

THORA.

I.

Trim and graceful, like a clipper, Thora was from
    top to toe,
Though her dress was very scanty and perhaps not
    comme il faut.
Bare and brown her little feet were, and her cheeks
    were sun-burnt too ;
But her lips were very rosy and her eyes were very
    blue.

One black skirt with red embroidery and a snowy
    white chemise
Were her wonted dress on week-days, when she felt
    herself at ease.
Hats she only wore in winter, when with snow the
    air was dim,
But her eyes peeped forth full brightly 'neath the
    big sou'wester's brim.

For who thinks that a sou'wester, e'en if e'er and
    e'er so wide,
From the boys' admiring glances could a pretty
    maiden hide?
And 'tis known how such attention every pretty
    maid annoys;
And it was a thousand pities, Thora did not like the
    boys.

They were either rude and noisy, or too bashful and
    confused.
As for loving them! No, thank you; she would
    rather be excused!
And, besides, there were so many, stout and slender,
    short and tall;
How could she her choice determine, since she
    could not love them all?

Thus she spoke unto her mother, sitting in the even-
    ing's glow
In the shadow of the fish-nets, which were drooping,
    row on row,

From their stakes; while to the westward hung the
    sun so huge and red,
Tinged with flame the white-winged sea-birds, drift-
    ing idly o'er her head.

"Sooth to say, thy words are canny," said the good-
    wife with a sigh,
Glancing seaward to conceal the merry twinkle in
    her eye.
"Yet 'tis right young girls should marry; childless
    age brings no maid boon;
Beauty gone, in vain they hanker, fretting idly for
    the moon.

"Therefore I will tell thee, daughter, what 'tis wise
    for thee to do;
One maid, e'en if e'er so canny, never knows as
    much as two.
We will call the girls together from the valley's
    every part;
They shall choose among thy wooers him who is to
    own thy heart."

"O, what sport!" cried pretty Thora; "thanks to
    thee, my mother dear;
O, how gayly we shall chatter when no prying men
    are near.
Loved and cherished shall my name be by the
    maidens round about;
I shall cause no cheeks to wither and no pretty lips
    to pout."

II.

While the mountain-tops were rosy and with dew
    the grass was wet,
Thora hastened to the boat-house to repair the fish-
    ing-net.
Skipping, jumping, wild and wanton, danced she
    o'er the fields away,
Tossing to the sportive echoes many a bright and
    careless lay.

When the lads who boats were bailing heard the
    pretty Thora sing,
Joining hands they ran to meet her, throwing round
    the maid a ring.

"Now," they cried, with boist'rous laughter, " now
    we've surely caught thee, Miss :
Thou canst only buy thy freedom if thou give us
    each a kiss."

  Come and take it, lads," said Thora ; "here's my
    mouth and here's my hand.
Kiss, indeed ! Why don't you take it ? Modest,
    sooth, is your demand."
And when one stepped briskly forward, half embold-
    ened by her speech,
With a slap she sent him spinning, like a top, upon
    the beach.

With a peal of mocking laughter off she bounded
    like a hind,
And her loosened yellow tresses fluttered wildly in
    the wind ;
While the lad, abashed, bewildered, strolled away,
    with burning ears,
To compose his wounded feelings and avoid his
    comrades' jeers.

Now a gallant lad was Halvor, who in storm and
    billows' roar
Oft had steered his skiff securely close beneath the
    rocky shore ;
And the thought within him rankled with a dull and
    gnawing pain,
That a little maid had smote him whom he could
    not smite again.

And the roguish face of Thora haunted him by night
    and day ;
Half he feared that he must love her ; for his wrath
    had flown away.
Yet he could have cursed his folly, had not cursing
    been a sin ;
Why should he thus love a maiden who was neither
    kith nor kin ?

Strange to say, the little Thora, when her anger was
    at rest,
Found some queer, soft thoughts awaking dimly in
    her troubled breast.

Had she not too harshly punished an offence not
    rudely meant?
Could she hope for God's forgiveness who could
    rashly thus resent?

As for kissing, that was foolish—that's, of course, be-
    fore a throng;
Yet, in Scripture, people did it, so it scarcely could
    be wrong.
Had he only been discreeter—met her 'neath the
    sinking sun—
Well—in sooth—there is no knowing what she
    might not then have done.

Thus with doubt and passion battling, and by vague
    regrets distraught,
Shyly nursing tender yearnings which she dared not
    frame in thought,
On the beach alone she wandered, where in whis-
    pered pulses beat,
Drunk with sleep, the mighty ocean, heaving darkly
    at her feet.

Then it seemed—what odd illusion!—that her footsteps on the sand
Broke into a double rhythm, sharply echoing o'er
   the strand,
And she felt a shadowy presence in the moonlight,
   gaunt and dread,
Moving stealthily behind her, and she dared not
   turn her head.

Swiftly, wildly, on she hurried, and the cloud and
   moon and star
With a dumb phantasmal ardor sped along th'
   horizon's bar;
Till exhausted, panting, sobbing, and bewildered
   with alarm,
Prone she fell, but up was lifted lightly on her
   lover's arm.

"Thora," said he, stooping o'er her, "pardon if I
   caused thee fright;
But my heart was full to bursting—speak I must
   and speak to-night.

Silence, Thora, is so heavy, like a load upon the
    breast.
Sooth, I think thou hast bewitched me—I can find
    nor peace nor rest."

Thora half-way stayed her weeping, and the moon,
    who peeped askance
From behind her cloud, revealed the tearful bright-
    ness of her glance.
"Oh, thou wouldst not love me," sobbed she, "if
    thou knew'st how bad I am.
Once—I hung—a great live lobster—on the tail of—
    Hans—our ram."

Scarce I know how he consoled her, but ere long
    her tears were dried,
And 'twas rumored in the parish, though again it
    was denied,
That while all the moon was hidden—all except the
    golden tips—
There was heard a sound mysterious, as of softly
    meeting lips.

For the good-wife, mildly grumbling at the idle
 spinning-wheel,
Rose at length and trudged sedately, anxious for the
 daughter's weal,
Over stone and sand and tangle, where the fright
 ened plovers flew
Screaming seaward, and majestic skyward soared the
 silent mew.

And 'twas she who with amazement heard the soft,
 mysterious sound,
And 'tis said she shook and tottered, almost fainting
 on the ground.
Scarce her reason she recovered, if the wild report
 be true,
For she saw a queer-shaped figure which proved
 later to be two.

"Daughter," said she, not ungently, "I have sought
 thee in alarm,
Fearing, in the treacherous moonlight, thou perchance hadst come to harm;

Yet I hoped that I should find thee, though the night be dark and drear,
Knowing that thou lov'st to wander where no prying men are near."

Dumb, abashed stood little Thora, and her cheeks were flaming red ;
Nervously she twirled her apron, and she hung her pretty head ;
Till at length she gathered courage and she whispered breathlessly :
"Mother dear—I love him—truly, and he says—that he loves me."

"Lord ha' mercy on us, daughter!" solemnly the dame replied.
"I who have the maids invited that thy choice they might decide ;
For of men there are so many, stout and slender, short and tall—
How's a maid to choose among them, since she cannot love them all?"

Now, the moon, who had been hiding in a veil of
    misty lace,
Wishing to embarrass no one by the shining of her
    face,
Peeped again, in modest wonder, ere her cloud she
    gently broke,
And she saw the good-wife smiling as to Thora thus
    she spoke :

"Since thou now hast chosen, daughter—every bird
    must try his wings—
Tell me, how didst thou discover that thy heart to
    Halvor clings?"
"Well," she said, in sweet confusion, while her eyes
    grew big with tears,
"Thou wouldst scarcely—understand it—mother
    dear—I boxed his ears."

EARL SIGURD'S CHRISTMAS EVE., Etc.

EARL SIGURD'S CHRISTMAS EVE.

I.

Earl Sigurd, he rides o'er the foam-crested brine,
And he heeds not the billowy brawl,
For he yearns to behold gentle Swanwhite, the
    maid
Who abides in Sir Burislav's hall.

"Earl Sigurd, the viking, he comes, he is near!
Earl Sigurd, the scourge of the sea;
Among the wild rovers who dwell on the deep,
There is none that is dreaded as he.

"Oh, hie ye, ye maidens, and hide where ye can,
Ere the clang of his war-ax ye hear,
For the wolf of the woods has more pity than
    he,
And his heart is as grim as his spear."

Thus ran the dread tidings, from castle to hut,
Through the length of Sir Burislav's land,
As they spied the red pennon unfurled to the breeze,
And the galleys that steered for the strand.

II.

But with menacing brow, looming high in his prow
Stood Earl Sigurd, and fair to behold
Was his bright, yellow hair, as it waved in the air,
'Neath the glittering helmet of gold.

"Up, my comrades, and stand with your broadswords in hand,
For the war is great Odin's delight;
And the Thunderer * proud, how he laughs in his cloud
When the Norsemen prepare for the fight!"

And the light galleys bore the fierce crew to the shore,
And naught good did their coming forebode,
And a wail rose on high to the storm-riven sky
As to Burislav's castle they strode.

---

* The god Thor, the Norse god of war.

Then the stout-hearted men of Sir Burislav's train
To the gate-way came thronging full fast,
And the battle-blade rang with a murderous clang,
Borne aloft on the wings of the blast.

And they hewed and they thrust, till each man bit
 the dust,
Their fierce valor availing them naught.
But the Thunderer proud, how he laughed in his
 cloud,
When he saw how the Norsemen had fought!

Then came Burislav forth; to the men of the
 North
Thus in quivering accents spake he:
"O, ye warriors, name me the ransom ye claim,
Or in gold, or in robes, or in fee."

"Oh, what reck I thy gold?" quoth Earl Sigurd,
 the bold;
"Has not Thor laid it all in my hand?
Give me Swanwhite, the fair, and by Balder I swear
I shall never revisit thy land.

"For my vengeance speeds fast, and I come like
    the blast
Of the night o'er the billowy brine;
I forget not thy scorn and thy laugh on that morn
When I wooed me the maid that was mine."

Then the chief, sore afraid, brought the lily-white
    maid
To the edge of the blood-sprinkled field,
And they bore her aloft o'er the sward of the croft
On the vault of the glittering shield.

But amain in their path, in a whirlwind of wrath
Came young Harold, Sir Burislav's son;
With a great voice he cried, while the echoes re-
    plied:
"Lo, my vengeance, it cometh anon!"

III.

"Hark ye, Norsemen, hear great tidings: Odin,
    Thor, and Frey are dead,
And white Christ, the strong and gentle, standeth
    peace-crowned in their stead.

Lo, the blood-stained day of vengeance to the ancient night is hurled,
And the dawn of Christ is beaming blessings o'er the new-born world.

"See the Cross in splendor gleaming far and wide o'er pine-clad heath,
While the flaming blade of battle slumbers in its golden sheath.
And before the lowly Savior, e'en the rider of the sea,
Sigurd, tamer of the billow, he hath bent the stubborn knee."

Now at Yule-tide sat he feasting on the shore of Drontheim fiord,
And his stalwart swains about him watched the bidding of their lord.
Huge his strength was, but his visage, it was mild and fair to see;
Ne'er old Norway, heroes' mother, bore a mightier son than he.

With her maids sat gentle Swanwhite 'neath a roof
    of gleaming shields,
As the rarer lily blossoms 'mid the green herbs of
    the fields;
To and fro their merry words flew lightly through
    the torch-lit room,
Like a shuttle deftly skipping through the mazes of
    the loom.

And the scalds with nimble fingers o'er the sound-
    ing harp-strings swept;
Now the strain in laughter rippled, now with hid-
    den woe it wept,
For they sang of Time's beginning, ere the sun the
    day brought forth—
Sang as sing the ocean breezes through the pine-
    woods of the North.

Bolder beat the breasts of Norsemen—when amid
    the tuneful din
Open sprang the heavy hall-doors, and a stranger
    entered in.

Tall his growth, though low he bended o'er a twisted
    staff of oak,
And his stalwart shape was folded in a dun, un-
    seemly cloak.

Straight the Earl his voice uplifted : " Hail to thee,
    my guest austere !
Drain with me this cup of welcome : thou shalt
    share our Yule-tide cheer.
Thou shalt sit next to my high-seat* e'en though
    lowly be thy birth,
For to-night our Lord, the Savior, came a stranger
    to his earth."

Up then rose the gentle Swanwhite, and her eyes
    with fear grew bright ;
Down the dusky hall she drifted, as a shadow drifts
    by night.

---

* The high-seat (accent on first syllable), the Icelandic *hasaeto*, was the seat reserved for the master of the house. It was situated in the middle of the north wall, facing south.

"If my lord would hold me worthy," low she spake,
    "then grant me leave
To abide between the stranger and my lord, this
    Christmas eve."

"Strange, O guest, is women's counsel, still their
    folly is the staff
Upon which our wisdom leaneth," and he laughed a
    burly laugh;
Lifted up her lissome body with a husband's tender
    pride,
Kissed her brow, and placed her gently in the high-
    seat at his side.

But the guest stood pale and quivered, where the
    red flames roofward rose,
And he clenched the brimming goblet in his fingers,
    fierce and close,
Then he spake: "All hail, Earl Sigurd, mightiest
    of the Norsemen, hail!
Ere I name to thee my tidings, I will taste thy flesh
    and ale."

Quoth the merry Earl with fervor: "Courteous is thy speech and free:
While thy worn soul thou refreshest, I will sing a song to thee;
For beneath that dusky-garment thou mayst hide a hero's heart,
And my hand, though stiff, hath scarcely yet unlearned the singer's art."

Then the arms so tightly folded round his neck the Earl unclasped,
And his heart was stirred within him as the silvern strings he grasped,
But with eyes of meek entreaty, closely to his side she clung,
While his mighty soul rose upward on the billows of the song.

For he sang, in tones impassioned, of the death of Æsir* bright,
Sang the song of Christ the glorious, who was born a babe to-night,

* Æsir is the collective name for all the Scandinavian gods.

How the hosts of heaven victorious joined the anthem of his birth,
Of the kings the starlight guided from the far lands of the earth.

And anon, with bodeful glamour fraught, the hurrying strain sped on,
As he sang the law of vengeance and the wrath forever gone,
Sang of gods with murder sated, who had laid the fair earth waste,
Who had whetted swords of Norsemen, plunged them into Norsemen's breast.

But he shook a shower of music, rippling from the silver strings,
And bright visions rose of angels and of fair and shining things
As he sang of heaven's rejoicing at the mild and bloodless reign
Of the gentle Christ who bringeth peace and goodwill unto men!

But the guest sat dumb and hearkened, staring at
    the brimming bowl,
While the lay with mighty wing-beats swept the
    darkness of his soul.
For the Christ who worketh wonders as of old, so
    e'en to-day
Sent his angel downward gliding on the ladder of
    the lay.

As the host his song had ended with a last resound-
    ing twang,
And within the harp's dumb chambers murmurous
    echoes faintly rang,
Up then sprang the guest, and straightway down-
    ward rolled his garment dun—
There stood Harold, the avenger, Burislav's un-
    daunted son.

High he loomed above the feasters in the torch-light
    dim and weird,
From his eyes hot tears were streaming, sparkling
    in his tawny beard;

Shining in his sea-blue mantle stood he 'mid that wondering throng,
And each maiden thought him fairest, and each warrior vowed him strong.

Swift he bared his blade of battle, flung it quivering on the board:
"Lo!" he cried, "I came to bid thee baleful greeting with my sword;
Thou hast dulled the edge that never shrank from battle's fiercest test—
Now I come, as comes a brother, swordless unto brother's breast.

"With three hundred men I landed in the gloaming at thy shore—
Dost thou hear their axes clanking on their shields without thy door?
But a yearning woke within me my sweet sister's voice to hear,
To behold her face and whisper words of warning in her ear.

"But I knew not of the new-born king, who holds
    the earth in sway,
And whose voice like fragrance blended in the soar-
    ings of thy lay.
This my vengeance now, O brother: foes as friends
    shall hands unite;
Teach me, thou, the wondrous tidings, and the law
    of Christ the white."

Touched as by an angel's glory, strangely shone
    Earl Sigurd's face,
As he locked his foe, his brother, in a brotherly em-
    brace;
And each warrior upward leaping, swung his horn
    with gold bedight:
"Hail to Sigurd, hail to Harold, three times hail to
    Christ the white!"

NORWAY.

Winter has its icy crown
　　Pressed round Norway's temples hoary;
Midnight's sun has showered down
　　On her head its glory.

Time's swift waves their power broke
　　'Gainst her ancient rocks and bowlders;
And the sea its misty cloak
　　Flung around her shoulders.

But when easeful Summer sinks
　　O'er the gleaming fiords and valleys,
Bursts the wood-lake's wintry links
　　And the lily's chalice—

Oh, what throbbing life aglow!
　　Oh, how fair the birch and willow,
And the gulls that drift like snow
　　O'er the rippling billow!

NORWAY.

Giant-like the glacier looms,
   Seaward throws its branches mazy;
And on Winter's bosom blooms
   Fearlessly the daisy.

Lo! the wild, bright peaks that shine
   Through the clouds that veil their bosom,
At whose foot, 'mid birch and pine,
   Fragile lilies blossom!

Here it was where Frithjof gay
   Wooed King Belé's fair-haired daughter;
Here she sang the sweet, sad lay
   Which her love had taught her.

Hence those vikings sprung whose sword
   Waked the South from idle dalliance;
Who in Vineland's rivers moored
   Dauntlessly their galleons.

Now, alas! that age hath fled,
   Fled the spirit that upbore it.
Ah, but still doth midnight shed
   Flaming splendor o'er it.

And the fame which curbed the sea,
   Spanned the sky with runes of fire,
Now but rustles tremblingly
   Through the poet's lyre.

THE NIXY.*

She sat at the opened window,
　　And mused o'er an old romance;
And the glorious peal of the legend
　　Still held her soul in its trance.
And her heart was thronged with yearnings
　　That cried for utterance.

The world seemed so pale and dreary,
　　A vain and inglorious play;
The thundering heroes of old time
　　Had left it to fade and decay;
The radiant soul had departed
　　And left the inanimate clay.

---

* The Nixy (Necken), according to Norse superstition, is a male sprite who lives in the rivers and roaring cataracts, through whose brawl the alluring music of his harp is often heard. He frequently beguiles young maidens by his wondrous melodies, in which his longing for human love and fellowship is expressed.

She closed the dear book of her heroes,
    And down from her tower she sped,
Where the shivering leaves of the birches
    A lingering glamour spread.
Strange murmurs stole through the forest,
    Strange voices of warning and dread.

She stood at the brink of the river,
    And heard the loud waters fall;
Now rising with deafening thunder,
    And wrestling with clamorous brawl;
Now breathing a quivering whisper
    Adown o'er the rocky wall.

Anon o'er the darksome waters
    The shadows of midnight brood,
And the ghosts of a thousand legends
    Flit through the shuddering wood;
But still at the brink of the river
    The maiden, wondering, stood.

There was a strong soul in the waters,
    A soul grand, noble, and free—

For the yawning abysses panted
   With tremulous ecstasy—
Which rose with a misty fulness,
   Then burst into melody.

And hushed was the night-wind's murmur,
   And hushed seemed the cataract's roll,
While clear and airily trembling
   The tones through the forest stole.
They came like familiar voices,
   That soothe the unrest of the soul.

The hopes her young heart had cherished,
   The dreams of the days gone by,
The yearnings that throbbed in her bosom,
   Deep-hidden from mortal eye,
Had gained a voice in the music,
   And joyfully rose to the sky.

A tenderly luring sadness
   Abode in the mellow tone.
Ah, there was love and solace
   For a life that was drear and lone!

A leap in the dark, a brief flutter, —
   And darkly the waves hurried on.

Two men at morn sought the river;
   And lo! to the tree-roots clung
The form of a lifeless maiden,
   So wondrously fair and young.
"'Twas the Nixy," they said, "who allured her,
   Beguiling her heart with his song."

AN EVERY-DAY TRAGEDY.

    He sat in honor's seat,
And rapturous ladies gazed into his eyes.
She stood without, beneath the wintry skies,
    In snow and sleet.

    He spoke of Faith's decay;
The ladies sighed because he spoke so true.
She hid her face in hands frost-numbed and blue,
    But dared not pray.

    In church, in court, and street,
Men bowed and ladies smiled where'er he went.
She stole through life, by shame and hunger bent,
    With bleeding feet.

    Upon his wedding-day
She stood, with burning eyes that fain would weep,
And heard the dancers' tread, the music's sweep,
    Sound far away.

The bride so pure and true
He took unto himself in haughty mood;
And all the paltry world applauding stood,
Though well it knew;

The while in frost and snow
Half-clad she stood upon whose maiden breast
He pledged his faith, for love's supremest test,
In joy and woe.

THE ELF-MAIDENS.

I.

AND it was young Sir Hermod, in scarlet clad and gold,
Rode forth to woo fair Ragna, the maid of Kirtley Wold.

Swift through the castle-gate rang the hoof-beat of his steed;
Then struck with muffled rhythm o'er the greensward of the mead.

Now, hie thee, young Sir Hermod, nor pause, nor look askance,
For 'neath the misty summer moon the elf-maidens dance.

And like a dream they drift o'er the silvery lakes of wheat,
The slender ears scarce dip 'neath the pressure of their feet.

They lightly sway and rock in their undulating flight,
With gleams of dimpling limbs and of bosoms of delight.

Now from the grove they float, and across the meadow's floor,
Scarce nod the drooping blue-bells when brush their garments o'er.

And from beneath the mist-veils that flutter in the dance
Grave, yearning eyes flash forth with a tender radiance.

O help thee God, Sir Hermod! Now spur thy goodly steed,
And list not to those sighs and the luring tones that plead.

Gaze not on snowy bosoms that in the moon's pale beam
Weave subtle charms, and strangely with lustrous dimness gleam.

That hand upon thy shoulder, so slender, soft and white,
Is Death's cold hand, outstretched thy fair youth and strength to blight.

Those soft, alluring voices that hover thee around,
Delicious, languid, vague, like a poppy's breath in sound,
Would lull thy soul full gently, amid the forest's gloom,
Into a sleep more dread than the slumber of the tomb.

Those locks that faintly glimmer—a maze of tawny gold—
Would tangle thee full swiftly in meshes manifold.

Those lips that blush so warmly beneath the moon's dim light
Would blot from out thy soul the dear name of Christ the white.

Then hie thee, young Sir Hermod, nor pause nor look askance,
Where 'neath the misty summer moon the elf-maidens dance.

II.

The winds that sang in tree-tops, and hummed the rose new-blown
Sweet airy tales, now swelled to a wild and wondrous moan.

Weird clouds with horrid faces, with fierce and breathless haste,
And sable arms extended, across the heavens chased.

The lily maid, fair Ragna, stood on the castle's height,
And watched the clouds and listened to the voices of the night.

She listened to the clang of swift hoof-beats from afar;
She heard the drowsy warden the heavy gate unbar.

And down the winding stairway with wingéd steps
    she flew—
The world was filled with music and all things fairer
    grew.

She cried her eager welcome to the knight who rigid
    sat ;
Nor stirred he in the saddle, nor raised his crested
    hat.

Then with a dread foreboding across the court she
    sped ;
She seized Sir Hermod's hand—but the hand was
    cold and dead.

She started back and tottered, but grasped the
    bridle's ring :
"Woe! Thou hast heard, belovéd, the elf-maidens
    sing.

"Now comfort Christ thy spirit, bestead in evil
    chance,
For thou hast seen at even-tide the elf-maidens
    dance."

NORSE STAVES.

INTRODUCTION.

Where under the pine-clothed mountain-side
    The glittering fiord lies dreaming,—
Where the sunlight plays with the sparkling tide,
    From the distant glaciers beaming,—

Where the midnight sun pours its flaming gold
    O'er the Yokul's airy steeple,
There lingers an echo from Saga old
    In the hearts of the Norseland people.

At the wedding-feast, when the home-brewed ale
    Has made its round of the table,
And the healthful mirth of a jocund tale
    Shakes the house from cellar to gable,

Then waketh again what hath slumbered so long,—
    The fire of the ancient Saga;
And the Norseman's heart flows over in song,
    As of old, at the goblet of Braga.

Full oft then a youth leaps forth from the crowd
    'Mid the dance and the music and laughter,—
Leaps forth with a shout so free and loud
    That it rings from rafter to rafter,—

And calleth a maiden out of the throng,
    And round them the revellers and dancers
Are hushed, while his heart pours forth its song,
    And the heart of the maiden answers.

STAVE IN "GUNNAR."

He. THERE standeth a birch in the lightsome lea—
She. In the lightsome lea;
He. So fair she stands in the sunlight free—
She. In the sunlight free.
Both. So fair she stands in the sunlight free.

She. High up on the mountain there standeth a pine—
He. There standeth a pine;
She. So stanchly grown and so tall and fine—
He. So tall and fine.
Both. So stanchly grown and so tall and fine.

He. A maiden I know as fair as the day—
She. As fair as the day;
He. She shines like the birch in the sunlight's play—
She. In the sunlight's play.
Both. She shines like the birch in the sunlight's play.

She. I know a lad in the spring's glad light—
He. In the spring's glad light;
She. Far-seen as the pine on the mountain-height—
He. On the mountain-height.
Both. Far-seen as the pine on the mountain-height.

He. So bright and blue are the starry skies—
She. The starry skies;
He. But brighter and bluer that maiden's eyes—
She. That maiden's eyes.
Both. But brighter and bluer that maiden's eyes.

She. And his have a depth like the fiord I know—
He. The fiord I know;
She. Wherein the heavens their beauty show—
He. Their beauty show.
Both. Wherein the heavens their beauty show.

He. The birds each morn seek the forest glade—
She. The forest glade;
He. So flock my thoughts to that lovely maid—
She. That lovely maid.
Both. So flock my thoughts to that lovely maid.

She. The moss, it clingeth so fast to the stone—
He. So fast to the stone;
She. So clingeth my soul to him alone—
He. To him alone.
Both. So clingeth my soul to him alone.

He. Each brook sings its song, but forever the same—
She. Forever the same;
He. Forever my heart sings that maiden's name—
She. That maiden's name.
Both. Forever my heart sings that maiden's name.

She. The plover hath but an only tone—
He. An only tone;
She. My life hath its love, and its love alone—
He. Its love alone.
Both. My life hath its love, and its love alone.

He. The rivers all to the fiord they go—
She. To the fiord they go;
He. So may our lives then together flow—
She. Together flow.
Both. So may our lives then together flow.

COME, FAIREST MAID.

He. "Come, fairest maid, tread the dance with me;
     O heigh ho!"
She. "So gladly tread I the dance with thee;
     O heigh ho!"
He. Like brier-roses thy red cheeks blush;
She. And thine are rough like the thorny bush.
    Both. An' a heigh ho!

He. So fresh and green is the sunny lea;
     O heigh ho!
She. The fiddle twangeth so merrily;
     O heigh ho!
He. So lightly goeth the lusty reel,
She. And round we whirl like a spinning-wheel.
    Both. An' a heigh ho!

COME, FAIREST MAID.

He. Thine eyes are bright like the sunny fiord;
     O heigh ho!
She. And thine do flash like a viking's sword;
     O heigh ho!
He. So lightly trippeth thy foot along;
She. The air is teeming with joyful song.
    Both. An' a heigh ho!

He. Then, fairest maid, while the woods are green,
     O heigh ho!
She. And thrushes sing the fresh leaves between,
     O heigh ho!
He. Come, let us dance in the gladsome day,
She. Dance hate, and sorrow, and care away.
    Both. An' a heigh ho!

TELL ME, ILKA.

He.   Tell me, Ilka on the hill-top,
       While the Alpine breezes blow,
       Are thy golden locks as golden
       As they were a year ago?
(Yodle)   Hohli-ohli-ohli-ho!
          Hohli-ohli-ohli-ho!   Hohlio-oh!

She.   Tell me, Hänsel in the valley,
       While the merry cuckoos crow,
       Is thy bristly beard as bristly
       As it was a year ago?
          Hohli-ohli-ohli-ho!
          Hohli-ohli-ohli-ho!   Hohlio-ho!

He.   Tell me, Ilka on the hill-top,
       While the crimson glaciers glow,
       Are thine eyes as blue and beaming
       As they were a year ago?
    Both. Hohli-ohli, etc.

TELL ME, ILKA.

She. Hänsel, Hänsel in the valley,
    I will tell you, tell you true;
    If mine eyes are blue and beaming,
    What is that, I pray, to you?
      Both. Hohli-ohli, etc.

He. Tell me, Ilka on the hill-top,
    While the blushing roses blow,
    Are thy lips as sweet for kissing
    As they were a year ago?
      Both. Hohli-ohli, etc.

She. Foolish Hänsel in the valley,
    Foolish Hänsel, tell me true,
    If my lips are sweet for kissing,
    What is that, I pray, to you?
      Both. Hohli-ohli, etc.

He. Tell me, Ilka on the hill-top,
    While the rivers seaward flow,
    Is thy heart as true and loving
    As it was a year ago?
      Both. Hohli-ohli, etc.

She. Dearest Hänsel in the valley,
I will tell you, tell you true :
Yes, my heart is ever loving,
True and loving unto you !
Both. Hohli-ohli-ohli-ho !
Hohli-ohli-ohli-ho !   Hŏhlio-oh!

SONNETS.

JUNO LUDOVISI.

I.

WHITE, silent goddess, whose divine repose
Shames the shrill ecstasies of later creeds,
What might is in thy presence that it breeds
This calm and deep delight that neither knows
Regret for past nor fear of coming woes!
I feel thee like a stately monotone,
Whose soundless waves against my spirit thrown
Make strong and pure. I feel the joy that flows
Like mild, unceasing rain upon my sense
From Nature's myriad fountains. In my soul
The lusty pagan wakes and roams the dense
Arcadian shades, and hears the distant roll
Of mingling echoes,—hears as in a dream
The cymbal's clash, the wild bacchante's scream.

II.

Sublime the thought that dwells within this stone
Imprisoned, yet immortal in its tomb.
Where since the world emerged from Chaos' womb
Was peace so sacred and so perfect known?
A spirit from some high ethereal zone,
A spirit pure and passionless and free,
Has flushed thy snowy immobility
With an intenser life-blood than his own.
In thy majestic womanhood more fair
Thou art than all the weeping horde of saints
Whom men invoke with incense and with prayer.
I in thine ear benign would breathe my plaint;
Before thy tranquil eyes and in the shade
Of thine eternal brow my sorrows fade.

III.

Come, gentle mother, and resume thy sway!
Lift up the mellow splendor of thine eyes.
Awake the dumb and callous earth that lies
Steeped in reluctant sleep. Send forth the gay
Olympian throng that, vanquished, fled away
When the pale King of Sorrows conquering came
From out the East. Within thy mighty frame
New life is kindling for a holier day.
For hark! Methinks within this gurgling stream
The Naiad's silvery voice I faintly hear;
Among the leaves I catch the fleeting gleam
Of white limbs vanishing; yea, far and near
Strange whispers haunt my sense, and tenderly
The hamadryad's pulse beats in this tree.

EVOLUTION.

I.

Broad were the bases of all being laid,
On pillars sunk in the unfathomed deep
Of universal void and primal sleep.
Some mighty will, in sooth, there was that swayed
The misty atoms which inhabited
The barren, unillumined fields of space;
A breath, perchance, that whirled the mists apace,
And shook the heavy indolence that weighed
Upon the moveless vapors. Oh, what vast,
Resounding undulations of effect
Awoke that breath! What dizzying æons passed
Ere yet a lichen patch the bare rock flecked!
Thus rolls with boom of elemental strife
The ancestry e'en of the meanest life.

II.

I am the child of earth and air and sea!
My lullaby by hoarse Silurian storms
Was chanted; and through endless changing forms
Of plant and bird and beast unceasingly
The toiling ages wrought to fashion me.
Lo, these large ancestors have left a breath
Of their strong souls in mine, defying death
And change. I grow and blossom as the tree,
And ever feel deep-delving earthy roots
Binding me daily to the common clay.
But with its airy impulse upward shoots
My life into the realms of light and day;
And thou, O Sea, stern mother of my soul,
Thy tempests sing in me, thy billows roll!

III.

A sacred kinship I would not forego
Binds me to all that breathes; through endless strife
The calm and deathless dignity of life
Unites each bleeding victim to its foe.
What life is in its essence, who doth know?
The iron chain that all creation girds,
Encompassing myself and beasts and birds,
Forges its bond unceasing from below,—
From water, stone, and plant, e'en unto man.
Within the rose a pulse that answered mine
(Though hushed and silently its life-tide ran)
I oft have felt; but when with joy divine
I hear the song-thrush warbling in my brain,
I glory in this vast creation's chain.

IV.

I stood and gazed with wonder blent with awe
Upon the giant foot-prints Nature left
Of her primeval march in yonder cleft:
A fern-leaf's airy woof, a reptile's claw,
In their eternal slumber there I saw
In deftly-wrought sarcophagi of stone.
What humid tempests, from rank forests blown,
Whirled from its parent stem yon slender straw?
What scaly creature of a monstrous breed
Bore yonder web-foot through the tepid tide?
Oh, what wide vistas thronged with mighty deed
And mightier thought have here mine eyes decried!
Come, a fraternal grasp, thou hand of stone!
The flesh that once was thine is now mine own.

V.

Sublime is life, though in beginnings base
At first enkindled. In this clod of mold
Beats with faint spirit-pulse the heart of gold
That warms the lily's cheek ; its silent grace
Dwells unborn 'neath this sod. Fain would I trace
The potent mystery which, like Midas' hand,
Thrills the mean clay into refulgence grand ;
For, gazing down the misty aisles of space
And time, upon my sight vast visions throng
Of the imperial destiny of man.
The life that throbbed in plant and beast ere long
Will break still wider orbits in its van,—
A race of peace-robed conquerors and kings,
Achieving evermore diviner things.

TO BAYARD TAYLOR.

(Dedication of a Biography of Goethe.)

Unto those altitudes of thought where day
Reigns e'er serene, where unrelenting law
Guides circling worlds and growth of tiniest straw,
Thou led'st with prescient step my doubting way.
And from those radiant heights where naught could
    stay
The daring eye, there burst upon my view,
Uplooming 'gainst eternity's vast blue,
The image of the mighty sage. The gray,
Forgotten ages spread about his throne
As if his lofty solitude to guard,
And large, eternal voices—Nature's own—
Spoke to the wakeful senses of her bard.
Here have I traced the record of his fame ;
Let me inscribe it, friend, with thy dear name.

I.—THE SEA.

CREATOR and destroyer, mighty sea!
   That in thy still and solitary deep
   Dost at all being's base thy vigil keep,
And nurturest serene and potently
The slumbering roots of vast Creation's tree.
   The teeming swarms of life that swim and creep,
   But half aroused from the primordial sleep—
All draw their evanescent breath from thee.
The rock thou buildest, and the fleeting cloud;
   Thy billows in eternal circuit rise
Through Nature's veins, with gentle might endowed,
   Throbbing in beast and flower in sweet disguise;
In sounding currents roaming o'er the earth
They speed th' alternate pulse of death and birth.

II.—THE AIR.

Invisible enchanter, sweet and strong,
    That crumblest mountains in thy soft embrace,
    That rock'st the feathered seed through sunlit space
And lull'st the sea with thy caressing song ;
How lightly dost thou dance the waves among,
    And wingest them for flight of fitful grace,
    And in the cloud-rack's path which none can trace
Dispersing cheer the parchéd earth along !
My voice thou bearest over dale and hill
    And spread'st in viewless billows near and far ;
And with a subtler undulation still
    Thou tremblest with the light of farthest star,
And holdest lightly, hovering on high,
The bright phantasmal bridge from earth to sky.

… TO LILLIE.

I SAT AND GAZED INTO THE BURNING SKY.*

I.

I sat and gazed into the burning sky
Where, like a dying king, the parting day,
In calm, majestic prescience of decay,
Lighted his pyre that he a king might die.
And I, whose thought upsoars on wider wings,
Since thy pure soul has breathed into my life
A quickened kinship with diviner things—
I builded there, remote from din and strife,
A spacious solitude, where thou and I
Might reign untroubled by the pace of time.
How with thy fleetest wish the cloud would thrill,
And, like some sweet, unmeditated rhyme,
Bend with melodious impulse to thy will!
And I, strong in thy love, unquailingly
Would greet the gaze of dread eternity.

* The author is well aware that this poem is not a sonnet, but as he cannot change it without ruining it, he prefers to print it as it is.

I SAW THE LILY PALE AND PERFECT GROW.

II.

I saw the lily pale and perfect grow
Amid its silent sisters in the mead.
Methought within its chilly depth to read
A maidenly severity, as though
A cool young life lay slumbering in the snow
Of its frail substance.   In that chalice white
Whose fairy texture shone against the light
An unawakened pulse beat faint and slow.
And I remembered, love, thy coy disdain,
When thou my love for thee hadst first divined;
Thy proud, shy tenderness—too proud to feign
That wilful blindness which is yet not blind.
Then toward the sun thy lily-life I turned—
With sudden splendor flushed its chalice burned.

WITHIN THE ROSE I FOUND A TREMBLING TEAR.

III.

Within the rose I found a trembling tear,
Close curtained in a gloom of crimson night
By tender petals from the outer light.
I plucked the flower and held it to my ear,
And thought within its fervid breast to hear
A smothered heart-beat throbbing soft and low.
I heard its busy life-blood gently flow,
Now far away and now so strangely near.
Ah, thought I, if these silent lips of flame
Could be unsealed and fling upon the air
Their woe, their passion, and in speech proclaim
Their warm intoxication of despair;—
Then would I give the rose into thy hand;
Thou couldst its voice, beloved, not withstand.

HOW CAN I LIGHTLY SPEAK THY WONDROUS NAME.

IV.

How can I lightly speak thy wondrous name,
Which breathes the airy fragrance of thyself,
As might, far straying from his flower, the elf
Hold yet a breath within his fragile frame
Of the flower's soul, betraying whence he came?
I too, beloved, though we stray apart,
Since in the vestal temple of thy heart
I dwell secure, glow with a sacred flame.
A breath of thy sweet self unto me clings—
A wondrous voice, as of large unborn deeds,
With deep resoundings through my being rings,
And unto wider realms of vision leads.
And dead to me are sorrow, doubt, and pain;
The slumbering god within me wakes again.

AN ANXIOUS WHISPER STEALS UNTO MY EAR.

v.

An anxious whisper steals unto my ear,
That thy young soul, so fresh and pure it be,
Is alien unto mine; that I in thee
No resonance shall find for thoughts austere;
No glorious kinship in that loftier sphere
Where spirits meet and recognize their own.
And yet, beloved, from those depths unknown—
Those slumbering depths of silence which I fear
With my rude touch to stir—some shy sweet
    thought
Comes upward trembling, like a coral bright,
Which no bold eye its loveliness has taught,
Through pale green waters flashing its warm light!
Yet, wert thou shallow, love, the heaven's wide
    sweep
The shallow stream reflects, e'en as the deep.

THY GRACIOUS FACE I GREET WITH GLAD SURPRISE.

VI.

Thy gracious face I greet with glad surprise
With each new day; and yet thou saidst a fear
Oft nestled at thy heart when I was near,
Because I loved thee only with mine eyes.
Thou wert not skilled in lore, nor deep, nor wise,
But thou wert strong to love and warm and true.
What could I answer, love? Alas, I knew
I love too well, perhaps, the radiant guise
Through which thy spirit breathes its loveliness.
Yes, darling, yes, I love thee as thou art,—
Thy coy surrender to my bold caress;
When folded in my arms, I feel thy heart
Beat 'gainst my breast; and when my lips meet thine
Thy very soul is wedded unto mine.

YES, MY OLD SELF IS DEAD; AND IT IS WELL.

VII.

Yes, my old self is dead; and it is well;—
I knew, as thou, he had no right to be;
And light his death was, for he knew not thee.
And thrilling into life by some strange spell
I stood new-born and wondering; nor could tell
Aught of what had been. Through a mist outspread
I saw the by-gone years lie cold and dead,
And the bright future where with thee I dwell,
A happy Delos rising from the sea.
Dim seems my past and strange, and all the earth
A pale and melancholy pageantry,
Until the shining moment of thy birth.
Thy life from out this age of toil and gloom
Sprang, like a flower that blossoms on a tomb.

IF I SHOULD LOSE THEE, DARLING, AND BEHOLD.

VIII.

If I should lose thee, darling, and behold
No more thy pallid brow, thy gentle eyes,—
This still unvanquished thought in wondrous guise
Returns to haunt me. On a cloud of gold
Amid the shining vastness of the spheres
I saw thee standing, while with helpless tears
I clung unto thy feet. The huge globe rolled
With strident noises onward, and the bright
And void, compassionless eternity
Beat with its deepening vistas on my sight;
When, lo! my hands wherewith I clung to thee
Grew weak, and with a speed no eye could trace
I sank through all the barren realms of space.

I SAW THEE DRIFTING, DRIFTING FAR AWAY.

IX.

I saw thee drifting, drifting far away,
And fading slowly on my famished eyes,
Like as a star that in the sun-bathed skies
Grows faint and flickers with unsteady ray;
Till 'mid the bright expanses of the day
Its slender life is quenched. "Oh, thou art lost
To me, and on this aimless whirlwind tossed
My wandering soul forevermore will stray,
Forever seeking thee, forevermore!"
Thus in the depth of my despair I cried,
And echoes from some sounding planet bore
My voice, on trembling pinions, far and wide.
Then desolation round about me spread,
Until methought that God himself was dead.

I WONDER OFT WHY GOD, WHO IS SO GOOD.

X.

I WONDER oft why God, who is so good,
Has barred so close, so close the gates of death.
I stand and listen with suspended breath
While night and silence round about me brood,
If then, perchance, some spirit-whisper would
Grow audible and pierce my torpid sense.
And oft I feel a presence, veiled, intense,
That pulses softly through the solitude ;
But as my soul leaps quivering to my ear
To grasp the potent message, all takes flight,
And from the fields and woods I only hear
The murmurous chorus of the summer night.
I am as one that's dead—yet in his gloom
Feels faintly song of birds above his tomb.

CALPURNIA.

CALPURNIA.

I.

PRELUDE.

Hot was the noon and heavy. A pitiless, quivering brightness
Hung in the motionless air ; and o'er the abodes of the Cæsars
Broke the fierce breath of the sun from the fathomless deeps of the heavens.
Tiber, the ancient, had shrunk in his bed, and, with sluggish pulsations,
Languished his tawny blood in his veins as he crept 'neath the arches,—
Crept 'neath the walls of the city of Mars to the happy Campagna.
Gray was the grass on his banks, and the far-spreading crowns of the palm-trees

Hung with a nerveless droop. Among the rank-
 growing rushes
Stirred no murmuring breeze; and, hid in the gloom
 of the ilex,
Moped the voiceless birds. Beneath the arcades of
 the temples
Brooded the spirit of silence; around the sculptured
 altars
Drowsed in the wide and tenantless space the heavy-
 eyed augurs,
Waiting in vain for the worshippers' tread and the
 prayers of the faithful,
Offering votive gifts on the shrines of the lofty Immortals.
Lo! without, on the Forum the stately façades and
 the columns
Lifted their snowy shapes against the deep blue of
 the ether,
Grave and placid, and pure, like the thought of a
 god of Olympus
Swiftly congealed to stone in its large, primeval per-
 fection.

Soundless and white was the noon; and, under the
    resonant arches,
Rose in trembling wavelets the air from the sun-
    smitten pavements,
And a bright lizard, perchance, that noiselessly slid
    o'er the marble,
Flashed his golden-brown throat, and a hound slunk
    by in the shadow,
Sadly, with lolling tongue. Thus desolate, silent,
    and weary,
Slept the great city at noon, the city of Mars and the
    Cæsars.

II.

IN THE PALACE OF THE CÆSARS.

High on the Palatine Hill, within the cool courts of
    his palace,
Stretched on the tawny skin of a beast from the
    African jungles,
Lay Maxentius Cæsar, the scourge of the angry Im-
    mortals.

Huge was his frame and seamed with the scars of
  manifold battles;
Rough-hewn his face and uncouth. A savage, bar-
  barian cunning
Lurked in his keen black eyes 'neath the bulging
  wall of his forehead,
Furrowed across with a blood-red streak from the
  rim of the helmet.
Bearded, burly, and fierce, like the men from Teu-
  tonian forest:
Such was Maxentius Cæsar. In Diocletian's ab-
  sence,
Held he the sceptre of Mars and ruled the realm of
  the Romans.
Close to the Emperor's couch, where the whispering
  spray of the fountains
Fell with its cooling breath from the tortuous horns
  of the Tritons,
Stood, in posture of greeting, Ausonius Mycon, the
  prætor;
Tall and noble his growth, and his face was clear as
  Apollo's.

"Wroth are the gods," quoth Cæsar. "Great Jove from the high-vaulted heavens
Thunders in cloudless space, but sends no rain to refresh us.
Parched is the land, and the fruits of the earth are sapless and withered.
Have I not harkened unto the voice of the priests and the augurs
Spying dark omens and signs amid the firmament's arches—
Bulls with flaming horns that dashed through the glittering star-world,
Black-winged birds that filled with their screams the heavens at midnight?
And in the steaming entrails of sacrificial cattle
Ill-boding signs have appeared. The maids of the virginal Vesta,
Late at their shuddering watch by the sacred fire of the goddess,
Thrice have swooned with dread, and terrible visions affright them.
Wroth are the gods; for they brook not the impious worship of Jesus

Risen (they say) from the dead,—a Galilean impos-
    tor,—
Brook not the presence of men who sleepless walk
    in the darkness,
Plotting disaster and death to the city of Mars and
    the Cæsars—
Who, in the stillness of night, with horrid rites of
    the Orient
Stain the fair face of the earth. The gods in their
    vengeance have wakened,
And, at the games which to-morrow will gather the
    flower of the Romans
Densely about the arena, the foes of the lofty Im-
    mortals
Shall with the reeking dust of the earth which their
    feet have polluted
Mingle their blood; and Death's keen tooth shall
    sting through their entrails."

Thus in wrath spoke Cæsar; Ausonius Mycon, the
    prætor,
Lifted his mournful eye, but tamed his tongue, for
    he dared not

Free the tumultuous thoughts which wrestled with
 might in his bosom.
And as he wavering stood he beheld, 'mid the blooming acacias
Which close-clustering grew at the brimming marge
 of the fountains,
Shyly a maiden approaching—a child of delicate
 stature.
Summers twelve had she told; like a bud-imprisoned
 blossom
Struggled her virginal grace through the tender
 beauty of childhood.
Pure was her brow, and her pallid cheek was wasted
 with weeping;
And in her eyes, where the gathering tears hung
 mute and appealing,
Lay something strange and remote, like the glow of
 a deep inspiration.
Wrapped was her slender form in a snowy garment
 that rippled
Down to her sandaled feet, and shone with glittering
 brooches

Artfully wrought into nodding doves that gleamed
    on her shoulders.
Warily trod she with timorous step on the glittering
    pavement,
Paused in fear at the shafts of the jasper and por-
    phyry columns,
Then more boldly advanced through the perfumed
    twilight that lingered
Under the marble arcades where reposed Maxentius
    Cæsar.
Wondering sore in his mind, Ausonius Mycon, the
    prætor,
Gazed at the lily-white maid, and saw her tremble
    and shiver
Like as a charméd bird that feels the eye of the ser-
    pent,
Saw how her bosom shook with smothered sobs, as
    she prostrate
Flung herself at the Emperor's feet. Then her voice
    she uplifted—
Cried with a wild, sharp cry, as if wrung from a soul
    in despairing:

"Cæsar Maxentius, hear me! Oh, hear me, Maxentius Cæsar!
Give me death at thy hand! Oh, let me die, I implore thee!
Why has thou spared a life so worthless, so weak and unfaithful,
When thou throw'st to the beasts my father, my mother—forgive me,
Christ! and restore me my strength—my mother, my mother,
To be thrown to the beasts in the sight of the bloodthirsty people!
I was weak. I denied my Lord; but now I am stronger.
Now I have strength to avow Him; for hath He not said to the faithful:
'He that loseth his life for My sake'—yes, Lord, I will follow—
Walk through the terrible portal of Death to Thy glory eternal—
Walk with unflinching feet, though my flesh be weak and unwilling!

Take me, O Cæsar, now; for now I am brave and
    intrepid!
Take me ere I grow weak and my heart within me
    unsteady!"

Thus she cried and wept, and the voice of her weep-
    ing resounded
Wide through the marble halls; while the whisper-
    ing waters descended
Cool in showers of spray from the Naiad's cup, and
    the Satyrs,
Poised on tiptoe in heedless delight 'mid the bloom-
    ing acacias,
Scarcely felt the restraint of the stone which their
    joy made immortal.

Silently listened Cæsar; then knit his brow in dis-
    pleasure;—
Laughed a menacing laugh which boded ill for the
    maiden.
"Death thou demandest," quoth he, "and sav'st us
    the cost of the hunting;

Foolish bird, that fliest unsought to the claws of the
   eagle!
Sooth, ere to-morrow's noon thou wilt flutter in vain
   in his talons.
Take her, Ausonius Mycon, and see that her prayer
   be denied not."
Thus he spoke, and the prætor, Ausonius Mycon,
   made answer:
"Master," said he, "thy servant I am, and my law is
   thy bidding.
Yet, if ever I merited praise for aught I have done
   thee,
Give me this maid as my slave; for choked are the
   prisons already
With the disciples of Christ that will bleed in the
   Flavian arena
For the delight of the people. The gods are com-
   passionate, Cæsar,—
Are not athirst for the blood of a pale and shy little
   maiden,
Who, by affection beguiled and natural love of her
   kindred,

Trod unthinking their path. My two Egyptian
    dancers,
Graceful, endowed with a skill that passes all under-
    standing,
These will I give thee if thou wilt deign to accept
    from thy servant
What is already thine own." But, with a snort of
    impatience,
Shouted Maxentius: "Take her, and send thy
    Egyptian dancers,
Even to-day—dost thou hear?—for languor oppresses
    me sorely."
Stooping, the prætor uplifted the swooning form of
    the maiden
From the hard touch of the stone, and bore her out
    of the palace,
Through the exterior court, where brawled the dis-
    solute guardsmen,
Playing at dice and tossing the clinking sesterce of
    silver
On the mosaic floor, and sentries erect in the
    shadow

Moveless stood 'neath the vaulted arcades, half-
    absently tracing
Upward the arabesques gay whose bright and deli-
    cate tendrils,
Like fleet voices of joy for a moment caught and ar-
    rested,
Climbed in fanciful flight. But all unheeding the
    prætor
Sped through the desolate streets and the resonant
    void of the Forum,
While the faint rhythm of the maiden's heart that
    beat 'gainst his bosom
Filled his soul with an unknown peace and with ten-
    der compassion.
On the Quirinal Hill, not far from the Gardens of
    Sallust,
Loudly he knocked at the gate and entered a high-
    ceiléd dwelling ;
Placed the maid on a couch, and thus he gently ad-
    dressed her :
" Child, I see by thy garb that thou art free-born
    and gentle,

Sprung of patrician race, perchance, for thy bearing
  is noble.
Far be the thought from my heart to make thee a
  slave in my household.
Rather my child shalt thou be, and my daughters
  will comfort and soothe thee,
Till thy young soul shall rebound from its dark and
  morbid deflection
Back to its natural poise of healthful enjoyment and
  gladness.
But, till thy wound be healed, I ask no importunate
  question
Touching thy birth and thy name, but bide my time
  till thou comest
Like mine own child to my knee, and reposest con-
  fidence in me."

III.

IN THE FLAVIAN ARENA.

Pale through the azure expanse of the sky the moon
  was ascending ;
Like intangible snow its breath of silvery vapor

Softly fell through the fields of the air o'er the slumbering city.
Then, with tremulous gleam, the stars burst forth, and Orion
Shone with a frosty sheen, and a vague and luminous shimmer
Rained from the Milky Way. But pure, and ghostly, and solemn
Rose the stately façade of the temple of Jupiter Stator;
Hushed and empty beneath, as if touched with a chilly remoteness,
Lay the white square of the Forum, where loomed the Phocian column
High in the moon-bathed stillness. The sculptured arch of Severus
Glimmered palely amidst the temples of deified Cæsars;
While, 'neath the brow of the Palatine Hill, the vast Coliseum
Flung its mantle of gloom to hide the deeds of the darkness,

Wrought on this terrible day for the joy of a barbarous people.
Sheltered deep in the shade of those huge and cavernous portals
Stood, close pressed to the stone, a little quivering maiden.
Fearless she stood and with burning eyes through the iron-barred gate-way
Gazed at the sated beasts that yawning drowsed in the shadow,—
Drowsed or slunk with velveted tread o'er the star-lit arena;
Snuffing, perchance, as they went the mangled form of a martyr,
Sightless, that stared with insensible orbs to the moon-flooded heavens.
Trembling she stood, and hugged the rigid bars of the iron
Close to her breast; but her sense seemed dead, and feeling, she felt not.
Silence brooded about her; until at the mouth of the portal

Sounded the clank of a lance upon the pavement of
   lava.
Then she turned with a start, though she long had
   expected the signal,
Saw 'gainst the brightness without three men advancing to meet her—
One a youth in the garb of the far-famed imperial
   legion,
Rugged the others and clad in the humble attire of
   the freedmen.
"Glaucus, I thank thee," so spoke in a shuddering
   whisper the maiden;
"Christ, who seeth in secret, this kindly deed will
   requite thee.
Now unbar me the gate and bid these brethren
   await me
Here, in the gloom of this arch, until I have rescued
   the bodies
Safe from the fangs of the beasts, that piously we
   may commit them
Unto the consecrate earth. My soul is constant and
   fearless,

E'en though weak be the flesh.   Perchance may the
    Lord hold me worthy
Here to receive for the sake of His name the crown
    of the martyr;
Then return to our brethren, and bid them kneel at
    the altar
Breathing a prayer for the soul of their sorrowful
    sister, Calpurnia."
"Child, thou temptest the Lord," the soldier Glau-
    cus made answer.
" ' Let the dead bury their dead,' for thus the Mas-
    ter hath spoken;
Wheresoever they rest, His hand, O sister, will
    reach them."
"Glaucus," she said, " I am lonely, and yearn and
    weep for my mother.
Lo, my poor life is a smoking flax and a reed that is
    bruisèd.
Pray the good Jesus to quench the feeble spark of
    my being—
He hath no work upon earth for one that was weak
    and denied Him."

Heaving a sigh, the soldier undid the bolts and the
    barriers,
And with unfaltering feet Calpurnia passed through
    the gate-way,
Murmured the blessed name which protects from
    the powers of evil,
Feeling a new-born strength that gushed through
    her veins and her fibres;
While with loud-beating heart the soldier gazed
    from the portal:
"Ah, Christ Jesus defend her! Death's jaws are
    yawning before her!
Seest thou not the sleek beast that yonder lurks by
    the pillar,
Crouching now for the leap?—now leaping? My
    vision forsakes me!
Heavenly Lord, where art thou that thus—but my
    sense is delirious—
Brothers, support me! Great God! Unharmed
    she stands, and a halo
Beams from her sorrowful face! Now stoops she
    and tenderly gazes

Into the sunken eyes of a saint. Oh, hie thee, sweet
    sister!
Dangers untold encompass thy path! Behold how
    she raises
Full to the moon the prostrate form, and kisses the
    pallid
Lips of the dead. O brothers, make haste—why
    stand we inactive?
Quick, draw the bolts from the gate! Oh, why do
    ye linger?
Hush! How the air doth quake! The roar of the
    Libyan lion
Rolls with thunderous echoes around the empty
    arena.
Darkness gathers about me! The moon in the mist-
    flooded distance
Loses her light and fades. The stars grow dim and
    unsteady.
Hark! from afar a faint shriek—a groan! Ye an-
    gels, forsake her
Not in her hour of need! I tremble! What see ye,
    my brethren?

Aid mine unfaithful eyes! Do ye hear a choked
    supplication
Rise through the stillness of night? And footsteps
    methinks that draw nearer—
Now retreating again? What is that? On the
    brink of perdition
Totters my foot! For behold, do ye see in the
    seat of the Cæsars,
Yonder, above the black arch, the shape of a toga-
    clad Roman?
Lost! Just God, I am lost! Do ye see how he
    stares unaverted,
Fierce, at the void within, like a beast that is sated
    with murder?
He resembles, methinks, Ausonius Mycon, the
    prætor!
Lord, thou hast visited swiftly my sin and my weak-
    ness upon me!
Yet I shall tremble no more! I will tread where
    my Savior has trodden!"

Thus spake Glaucus, but ere his sad voice had ex-
    pired in the twilight,

Saw he Calpurnia stand at the portal and beckoning
  to him.
Pale she stood and erect, and her frame seemed frail
  and translucent,
As if the light of the radiant soul were shimmering
  through it ;
And at her feet, with withered lips and rigidly
  staring,
Lay her beloved dead ; and Glaucus, forgetting his
  terror,
Straightway unbarred the gate, that, grating, swung
  on its hinges,—
Lifted the lifeless clay of the saints, and tenderly
  placed them
Side by side on a bier, and hid their blood-sprinkled
  garments,
Hid their gaping wounds, 'neath a shroud of precious linen.
Seizing the bier the freedmen emerged from the
  gloom of the portal ;
Swiftly they moved through the night, and Calpurnia followed behind them,

Down the Appian Way and on through the Porta Latina.
Tearless and dumb she hurried away o'er the smooth-trodden pavement,
Feeling scarcely the weight of her limbs, nor the touch of the lava—
Feeling only a world of woe that throbbed in her bosom.
"Ah, little maid, thy grief makes thee blind, and thy vigilant senses
List to the tumult within and thy heart's tempestuous beating;
Dulled are thine ears to the muffled tread of sandaled footsteps—
Footsteps whose shadowy sound awakens no treacherous echo
From the dim gates of the tombs, where sleep the mighty departed.
Nor do thy fevered eyes descry in the gathering twilight
Something that steals through the mist, now tarries a while at the way-side,

Then, with a peering gaze and noiselessly, hasteneth
    onward,
Pausing when thou dost pause, and when thou advancest, advancing."

IV.

IN THE CATACOMBS OF ST. CALIXTUS.

HUSHED from the depths of the earth, with a sweet,
    ethereal cadence,
Came the soft strains of a song—a hymn of praise
    and of gladness:
"Blessèd," they sang, "are the dead who die in the
    Lord;" and a youthful
Voice, with the virginal dew of faith and childhood
    upon it,
Rose through the sod and hovered aloft like a joy-
    wingèd seraph:
"Blessèd and holy is he that hath part in the first
    resurrection."
Here, 'neath the boughs of a cypress copse, in the
    sheltering shadow

(Dense and opaque, like a hoar-frost of darkness
    congealed on the tiny
Spears of the vernal grass), Calpurnia paused, and
    the freedmen ;
Then, with a wary hand, she knocked on a stone
    that was hidden
Half in a jungle of roses that grew 'mid the roots of
    the cypress.
"Christ is risen," she said ; and the answer came to
    the watchword :
"Yea, He is risen, indeed ; " and lo ! the stone was
    uplifted
Quickly by arms from beneath ; and straightway
    clearer and tenderer,
Like a sweet face that is quickly revealed 'neath the
    veil that has hid it,
Burst the glad chant from the womb of the earth
    and soared to the heavens :
"Thou wilt show me the path of life ; behold in Thy
    presence,
Lord, there is fulness of joy." A moment's glare of
    the torches,

Flaming red in the gloom, but ghostly and white in
    the moonlight ;
Then a dull thud of the stone, as the martyred dead
    and the living
Vanished beneath it. Now ceased the chant, and in
    reverent silence
Bore they the saints to their rest through the long,
    subterranean chambers,
Haunted by shadowy watchers, and reached the cave
    where the brethren
Worshipped the Lord in prayer and song, while the
    white-haired bishop
Spoke the words of life to strengthen the weak and
    the weary,
Spoke to refresh the souls that drooping fell by the
    way-side.
When Calpurnia saw his mild, compassionate vis-
    age,
Forth she sprang, embracing his knees ; and as the
    smooth billow
Dumbly swells till it breaks on the strand in melodi-
    ous ripples,

Thus her imprisoned grief, that had mutely swelled
   in her bosom,
Burst in a shower of tears at the goal of her perilous
   wandering.
"Father," she cried, "the Lord hath turned His
   countenance from me!
Him I denied in my weakness, and now, in His
   wrath, He rejects me.
Cæsar I prayed for death, but he made me a slave.
   Oh, my father,
Even the Libyan lion that lurks in the Flavian
   arena
Harmed me not; so vile I am, and the Lord will
   not take me;
Lo, I went in this night to save the clay that was
   precious
Unto my heart from the impious hands of the base
   and ungodly.
Here I have brought it to thee; thou wilt bury my
   father and mother
Here in the hallowed soil where sleep generations
   of martyrs."

"Daughter," the patriarch answered, and murmured
    a soft benediction,
Placing his hands on her throbbing brow and sooth-
    ing her gently,
"Sooth, thou hast sinned in denying the Lord; but
    the Savior is gracious;
He has forgiven thy sin, for hard was thy self-im-
    posed penance.
Think not, child, that He has thrust thee away from
    His bosom;
If He withheld the martyr's crown in the bloody
    arena,
He has desired thee to live and, living, to further
    His kingdom."
"Oh, but my father," Calpurnia sobbed, "I am
    weak and unworthy!
What is the life of a maiden slave, that the Lord in
    His glory
E'er should bethink Him of her, and the flickering
    flame of her being
Shield with His mighty hands against the breath of
    destruction?

Father, oh pray that I die, for I am alone and am
 weary."
"Child," the bishop replied, "two sparrows are sold
 for a farthing ;
Yet falls not one to the ground without the will of
 Our Father.
Wondrous, indeed, are the ways of the Lord, and
 even thy weakness
He has preserved to work His will, though ob-
 scurely and blindly.
Death hast thou sought, and thou weepest that mar-
 tyrdom is denied thee ;
Life has its martyrs, my daughter, as brave, as
 strong, and as faithful,
E'en as the martyrs of death. And thine is the work
 of confession,
Not by thy blood, but by deeds of heroic meekness
 and patience.
Deeds of forbearance and kindness 'mid unending
 toil and injustice—
Deeds that calmly shall shine in the gloom which
 thy path shall encompass,

Like the small flame of a lamp that unsteadily glim-
    mers and flickers
Lone in the night, and showeth the gloom, though
    it cannot disperse it.
Christ has withheld the fangs of the beasts from thy
    delicate body,
Shielding thee, child, from the martyr's death, be-
    cause He will grant thee
That which, my daughter, is harder to bear—the life
    of a martyr."
Thus the patriarch spoke, and knelt in prayer at the
    altar
Close at Calpurnia's side, and all the brethren assem-
    bled
Bowed their heads in silence, and prayed for the
    souls of the martyrs
Summoned to stand this night before the face of the
    Savior,
Hearing the joyful words from His lips, "Ye blest
    of my Father,
Enter ye into the kingdom;" while in the dim light
    of the tapers

Gleamed on the wall indistinctly, an outline mosaic of Jesus,
Drawn as the Shepherd who bears the lamb that was lost on His shoulders.
Deep was the stillness, save for the crackle, perchance, of the torches,
Save for the smothered sobs of a maiden bereaved, or a widow,
Striving in vain to strangle her natural grief, and to follow
Upward her loved one in thought to his blessèd rest from his labors
Safe in the kingdom of God. Then suddenly from the watchers
Came a loud shriek of alarm, and, ere the brethren assembled
Woke from the rapture of prayer, beheld they standing among them—
Toga-clad, tall, and erect—Ausonius Mycon, the prætor.
"Stay, disciples of Christ!" he cried, and his sword he uplifted.

"Fear me no more, for alas! the strength of my
   arm—it is broken.
Here is my sword," and he flung the blade at the
   feet of the bishop.
"Wreak your vengeance upon me, for swordless
   stand I among you;
Red are my hands with the innocent blood of your
   fathers and daughters."
Half re-assured, yet fearful, the brethren paused in
   the door-ways,
Gazing over their shoulders with glances of doubt
   and suspicion,
While at the altar immovable stood the reverent
   bishop,
Grave and serene and pale at his feet lay the maid-
   en Calpurnia.
"Priest," the prætor resumed, "I know not the God
   whom thou servest;
Yet have I seen the strength He has given this pale
   little maiden;
Wondering sore have I heard the words which
   through thee He hath spoken.

Lo! I have waged against Him a vain, ineffectual
    warfare,
And by the deeds of this night I am utterly broken
    and conquered.
Late in the watches nocturnal I rose, and the light
    mists of slumber
Rubbed from mine eyes, and tracked this child
    through devious path-ways
Unto the Flavian arena. I hoped, perchance, to
    discover
Where in the womb of the night your hidden wor-
    ship eluded
Ever my vigilant search. I had not resolved to be-
    tray you,
But, by my knowledge armed, to keep you in bitter
    subjection.
Ah, but this shy little maid has vanquished her
    valiant pursuer!
Now he is fain to fall at her feet, and beg her to
    lead him
Unto that fountain of life whence spring such trust
    and devotion,

Courage so high and serene in the face of death and
    of danger,
Valor in frailty clad and strength thus wedded to
    weakness.
Therefore, the God whom Calpurnia serves, O
    priest, I will worship;
I and my household will bend our knees, bringing
    gifts to His altars;
Thou wilt teach us the wingèd ways that lead to His
    favor."
Silently burned in haloes of mist the delicate
    tapers,
Fell their pale sheen on faces upturned in prayerful
    rapture,
Fell on the reverent priest as he on the brow of the
    maiden
Rested his hands and blessed her, and spake in a
    tremulous whisper:
"Daughter, behold! 'tis the voice of the Lord hath
    given thee answer.
Now thou knowest the worth of the life which He
    has protected,

Hold it henceforth as His gift, that is left for a time
    in thy keeping.
Stake it not rashly in self-sought peril, but cherish it
    dearly!
Though in thy sight it seem worthless and mean, to
    Him it is precious.
Daughter, be faithful and brave and true to His
    merciful summons,
Wondrous results then may spring from the deeds
    of a weak little maiden."

Far was the night advanced, and the hour of morn
    was approaching,
Soon from the daylight world overhead came fitful
    and muffled
Sounds, as if heard through the mists of a dream
    with remote indistinctness;
Now the dull creak of a vintner's wain drawn by
    heavy-limbed oxen,
Now the sharp clank of a horse's hoof on the pave-
    ment of lava.
Straightway the bishop moved, preceded by minis-
    tering brethren,

Bearing torches and tapers, along the tenebrious
    path-ways,
Paused at an open tomb in the masoned wall of a
    cavern,
Placed the martyrs with prayer and chant in the
    coffins of marble,
Bearing the sign of the fish and the words: "*Requiescat in pace.*"
Then, by the torches led through the long, labyrinthine recesses,
Hastened the children of Christ to the upper
    abodes of the daylight.

One by one they emerged from the blossoming
    jungle of roses,
Shading their dazzled eyes and cautiously peering
    around them;
Quickly they spread o'er the fields, or toward the
    Porta Latina
Urged their steps and sought their accustomed
    haunts in the city.
Last of all, clad in civic attire, the bishop ascended,

And at his side with solemn brow went Ausonius Mycon,
Holding close to his breast the little maiden Calpurnia,
Who, from the terrible strain of the night and the wild agitation,
Lay as if wrapt in a swoon, so deep and calm was her slumber.
Angels with peace in their wings had gently breathed on her eyelids,
Blown the foot-prints of care from the sweet, unconscious features,
Till they relaxed again to their soft and infantine roundness,
Touched by the strange remoteness of sleep that rested upon them.
Gently the bishop clasped her listless hand, as he whispered,
Solemnly: " Prætor, behold, of such is the kingdom of heaven."
Close to the edge of the cypress copse, where the flame-chaliced poppies

Clustering grew, they watched the dawn as it dimly awakened,
Pale with tinges of rose that strayed o'er the crests of the mountains,
Ere with its fiery blush it fringed the hovering cloudlets,
Darting radiant shafts of dewy light and of color
Up 'mid the fleecy embankments of mist and of shivering vapors,—
Opening deeps in the sky whence the night was slowly receding,
Chilly vistas where lingered reluctant, cerulean shadows,
Dark with a tint as of steel; then elfin showers of sunlight
Quivered upward in roseate hues and spread to the zenith,
Till the gray west responsively flushed with a faint crimson pallor.

Long the patriarch stood and gazed at the vanguard of morning.

Touching the prætor, he said : "The kingdom of
    Christ is advancing
Silently, brightly, and calmly, as marches the con-
    quering daylight.
And to the hour of my death this glad conviction I
    cherish :
Surely the Lord will scatter the gloom of the night,
    and triumphant
Hurl the keen shafts of His truth into the shadows
    of error,
Lift the light of His visage upon the dwellers in
    darkness.
Mine the eyes that shall see this realm lie prostrate
    before Him."

www.ingramcontent.com/pod-product-compliance
Lightning Source LLC
Chambersburg PA
CBHW020245170426
43202CB00008B/235